W9-BKZ-986

THE
COUCH
AND THE
ALTAR

BOOKS BY DAVID A. REDDING

The Parables He Told
Psalms of David
The Miracles of Christ
If I Could Pray Again
The New Immorality
The Couch and the Altar

THE
COUCH
AND
THE
ALTAR

DAVID A. REDDING

J. B. LIPPINCOTT COMPANY
Philadelphia and New York

Theodore Lownik Library
St. Procopius College
Lisle, Illinois

200,19 5
R 3/3 C

Copyright © 1968 by David A. Redding

All rights reserved

First Edition

Printed in the United States of America

Library of Congress Catalog Card No.: 68–29729

The lines quoted from "Alone in the World" are copyright © 1962 by Chappell-Styne, Inc. Used by permission of Chappell-Styne, Inc.

The quotations from T. S. Eliot's *The Cocktail Party, The Family Reunion,* "Ash-Wednesday," "East Coker," and "Little Gidding" are used by permission of his publishers, Harcourt, Brace & World, Inc. All are included in *The Complete Poems and Plays, 1909–1950.*

The quotation from *Living under Tension* by Harry Emerson Fosdick is used by permission of Harper & Row, Publishers, Incorporated.

The material on pp. 24, 25 is from *The Basic Writings of Sigmund Freud,* trans. and ed. by Dr. A. A. Brill, copyright 1938 by Random House, Inc., copyright renewed 1965 by Gioia Bernheim and Edmund Brill. Reprinted by permission.

The quotation from "A Cabin in the Clearing" from *In the Clearing* by Robert Frost is copyright 1951, © 1962 by Robert Frost; that from "The Gift Outright" from *Complete Poems of Robert Frost* is copyright 1942 by Robert Frost. Reprinted by permission of Holt, Rinehart and Winston, Inc.

The lines quoted from *For Heaven's Sake!* (book and lyrics by Helen Kromer) are © 1961 by Helen Lenore Kromer and © 1963 (new material added) by Walter H. Baker Co. All rights reserved.

The passage from *Beyond Anxiety* by James Pike is quoted by permission of Charles Scribner's Sons.

The lines from *Psalms of David* by David A. Redding are quoted by permission of Fleming H. Revell Company.

The quotation from *Escape from Loneliness* by Paul Tournier is translated by John S. Gilmour, published by The Westminster Press, copyright © 1962 by W. L. Jenkins, and used by permission. The quotations from *The Strong and the Weak* by Paul Tournier are translated by Edwin Hudson, published in the U. S. A. by The Westminster Press, 1963, and used by permission. The quotations from *A Whole Person in a Broken World* by Paul Tournier are used by permission of Harper & Row, Publishers, Incorporated.

TO THE GLORY OF GOD

ACKNOWLEDGMENTS

Linda Gilbert Davis

Louise Allen Peters

Nancy Rail Daugherty

Dorothy McCleery Redding

John Maxwell McCleery, M.D.

Ben Schneider, Ph.D.

PREFACE: THE CONFESSOR AND THE ANALYST

YOU CAN BE freed from the darkest prison of problems and find your way to peace and happiness. The examples I have recounted in this book illustrate my growing conviction that no mountain is so huge that it cannot move over from on top of us. It is a mistake to be a Pollyanna, but what a pity to be morbid or mechanical about human nature. I myself have been repeatedly astounded at the spectacular results accomplished through love and understanding. And it has been difficult for me to come to a belief in *re*-creation. It was as though what I knew about therapy at first stood in the way. The very idea of someone saying "I feel like a new man" made me suspicious. I had to learn miracles the hard way. But I have now seen so many men and women who have come back after having been dismissed forever to the floor that I must insist with the poet, no matter what hurts you nor how long you have suffered: "Woe unto him who believes in nothing. Always the impossible happens."

However, both science and Scripture agree that this momentous change cannot come in your life until you first come to yourself. It is my hope that in these pages you may meet yourself through the experiences of others.

In my work as a church confessor and campus counselor I have learned to respect the immense contribution of Sigmund Freud and his successors to our quest for personal discovery. And yet Freud was the first to admit that, while science might bring relief, it was not to be misunderstood as a remedy for what ails human nature. To my mind, our only hope today, as at the dawn of Christian history, lies in the love of God alighting in our lives. It is time to appreciate the relevance of our most holy faith to the insights of modern psychology, and not be afraid to mention the evidence for the miraculous that shouts all around those of us who find ourselves to be believers.

I know of no word strong enough to describe what I have witnessed and what I wish for you except that often misused and misunderstood word, rebirth. Frankly, I know of nothing short of a religious experience that can handle our human predicament.

I remember a man with whom I had worked in vain in an effort to help him discipline his weakness. Repeatedly he fell apart in the time of temptation. Our therapy seemed futile to sustain his integration. Then we realized, as I have had to be reminded so many humiliating times, that his case was impossible—for man. We prayed about it together and alone all that summer.

One day he came radiant to tell me his dream of the previous night. He had always related the great blue heron in his mind with the centrifugal pull in his life that he knew he must overcome. In some way he had likened himself to a heron with a crippled wing, at least unable to fly away free from his burden. In his dream the heron swept into view and swooped down into an aperture in the rock at his feet. He waited breathless. In a moment, in a twinkling of an eye, out flew a beautiful winged horse, dapple-gray and powerful, soaring effortlessly off into a dazzling sky. The heron reborn as Pegasus announced a transformation in him equal to the demands his former self had failed to meet. It did not signify simply improvement but being made new. It was reminiscent of something Isaiah was trying to explain when he said: ". . . they that wait upon the Lord shall renew their strength; they shall mount up with wings as eagles; they shall run, and not be weary; and they shall walk, and not faint" (Isa. 40:31). A vulnerable bird had become a dynamic and winged horse.

Our rescue depends not simply in being able to put our fury and fears into tears and talk, as Freud found, but in finally reaching the place where we can give the healing forgiveness and receive the blessed strength. The wholeness we seek is not something that can be spooned out like an elixir to a reclining patient on a couch; rather, it is a grace anointing the pilgrim kneeling by his altar.

Psychiatry means literally "the healing of souls," and as surely as the church sorely needed Sigmund Freud's help in order to take a man apart and analyze his problems, so psychology must not lightly dismiss man's need of God to put a man back together to stay. Our need now may be not so much for psychoanalysis as it is for what Martin Buber calls "psycho-synthesis." It is the mission of this manuscript to bring the couch and the altar closer together for this purpose and to hasten the day when they will prove to be a happy combination.

Let the priest welcome the physician to the business in which he has failed alone, and let the physician respect the power of those ordained in the name of the Great Physician to restore men to their rightful minds. Freud excluded no one from his profession, but announced at the beginning of his first lecture in this country: "I have noticed with considerable satisfaction that the majority of my hearers do not belong to the medical profession. Now do not fear that a medical education is necessary to follow what I have to say."[1]

One of the major paths psychoanalysis has taken is now evolving into a position to which Christianity can grant its unqualified blessing. Freud's most distinguished student was the late Swiss physician and psychoanalyst, C. G. Jung. Jung

broke early with Freud's antireligious attitude, and across the
years of an incredibly long practice developed an approach
which he termed "analytical psychology." Jung's experience
made him a mystic and a profound believer in God. Contrary
to Freud, he found from his clinical experience that belief in
God and in immortality were as essential to a patient's psyche
as salt to his physique. Jung wrote in his *Modern Man in
Search of a Soul* that all of his patients over thirty-five years of
age fell sick because they had lost their faith in God or in the
future life. And he insisted that none of them were cured until
those basic emotional needs were met by religious faith. "It
happens sometimes," wrote Jung, "that I must say to an older
patient, 'Your picture of God or your idea of immortality is
atrophied; consequently your psychic metabolism is out of
gear.' "[2]

Jung brought psychotherapy a long way toward a position
which would be congenial to a Christian concept of man.
Christians cannot recommend that men go to just any psychoanalyst, any more than to just any preacher. Despite all
protestations to the contrary, a non-Christian counselor inevitably conveys his own convictions into such an intimate relationship, and the harm that is done, or the omissions made at
the crucial time the patient makes his integration, can scarcely
be remedied by the church later on at a less critical and less
formative period of the personality's development. Christians
cannot smile over the jeopardy in which a patient is placed if
he is encouraged to reorient around a wife or any god short of
the One who made him, as though he could take or leave God
according to his disposition. It is not poor sportsmanship if the
priest is uneasy about an anti- or unchristian counselor. A man
of God must view the building of any person's life on anything
less than rock as building upon sand. In Christian perspective,
provincial as it may appear, unless a man approaches an experi-

ence of God, his psychotherapy was only partial or patchwork. For, in Biblical light, a man's health as well as his sanity, even his capacity to relate to others as well as himself, are most profoundly dependent upon his relationship to God.

Counselors must meet Freud appreciatively to minister effectively, but not miss the correction offered, for instance, by such men as Martin Buber. Buber criticises Freudians for perpetuating a rigid dogma-centered psychotherapy and for freezing the doctor impersonally out of reach of the patient. Buber believes that the psychotherapist must risk a man-to-man meeting which makes the two partners in a mutual experience. The patient is not simply to recite his history to some remote mechanic encased in professionalism. Both are to embark upon a completely unrehearsed and unpredictable adventure that will risk salvation's only hope for them both.

My own experience also demonstrates that each consultation must be seen by itself—unprecedented and unclassifiable. And whatever results will come as a surprise and as an exchange, reminding the psychotherapist what a privileged fool he is, standing as he does inside the unfolding drama of raw creation. The counselor is no exterior fixture, but inhaled into the same theater of the absurd to be exposed repeatedly both as schoolboy and beneficiary, blest as bearing blessing.

Life is much livelier than either the psychiatric mechanic or stereotyped evangelist is prepared to discover. Men like Buber awaken us to the wonder of an unmanufactured life actually being recreated before our very eyes by a hand both mysterious and divine. "There is no sureness of expressible knowledge but the certainty of meeting what remains undisclosed."[3]

Carl Jung and Martin Buber are but a step away from the classic Christian position which is being taken seriously by some of their professional descendents and particularly exemplified by our contemporary, the Swiss psychotherapist, Dr.

Paul Tournier, who brings the couch completely into Christian context. Tournier explained in a recent address delivered at Oberlin College, "My *Médecine de la Personne*[4] combines the psychology of Jung and the faith of Tournier."

Dr. Tournier with marked humility has actually demonstrated in his long practice that he knows how to refer his patients to the Great Physician. It is an event of some significance to find a scientist of international repute, a physician who is held in high esteem by his colleagues in medicine, who confides that his psychotherapy began with his religious experience and not from his scientific training, which came later. For a physician to remind his own profession, as well as his friends in divinity, that nothing short of an experience of the grace of God can heal the patient, and that no doctor can assist another in that delivery without first possessing it himself, represents a new era in the marriage of medicine and faith.

Much of what we are now discovering about human nature and therapy has been there in Scripture waiting to be recovered. The definitive work on guilt may be the Thirty-second Psalm. You and I may not have dipped our hands in blood as brutally as our sister, Lady Macbeth, but there is endemic in the best man a "damned spot," a perversion really, that will not wash out by hand nor yield to the most sophisticated finesse of psychiatric medicine. And distinguished psychotherapists have at last arisen in our time to speak the lines of Lady Macbeth's physician to our own condition.

> This disease is beyond my practice:
> . . . infected minds
> To their deaf pillows will discharge their secrets;
> More needs she the divine than the physician.
> God, God forgive us all! Look after her; . . .
>   *Macbeth*, Act V, Scene I

This is the wise referral for which our sad and mutilated world is waiting and which is acknowledged so relevantly by the brilliant counselor in T. S. Eliot's play, *The Cocktail Party:*

> You are right, Mr. Chamberlayne
> You are no case for my sanatorium
> You are much too ill.

Experts still know little more about the mind than men knew about the globe before Columbus, but in time to come Christians will look back upon today as the crucial time when the Freudian couch and the Christian altar were reconciled.

Now we shall examine how all this applies to you and me.

DAVID A. REDDING

St. Augustine, Florida

CONTENTS

Preface: The Confessor and the Analyst   7

1   Who Am I?   *17*

2   Who Was I?   *27*

3   Resentful?   *41*

4   Guilty?   *53*

5   Lonely?   *67*

6   Weak?   *81*

7   Afraid?   *93*

8   Yes.   *103*

9   What Will Become of Me?   *113*

Notes   *123*

1
WHO AM I?

WHO AM I? I am many things others can clearly see but I cannot yet bear to hear, to say nothing of accept. I have emotional blocks, perhaps an acute dread of heights or confinement. These are clues to me, my problems, doorways to self-understanding. In me is a pleasure-mad *id*, and added to my ego, "the conscience of the unconscious." There is so much more to you and me than most men are willing to imagine. We are only beginning to learn the alphabet of this vast subterranean stretch of self which must also be saved.

Who are you? We do not know each other very well. Our conflicting impressions of familiar celebrities and political candidates betray us as no judges of human nature. King David's character is still held in dispute. We cannot even agree on Jesus Christ: "But who do you say that I am?" (Mark 8:29; Luke 9:20). Our concept of our closest friend is likely a case of mistaken identity. Except for superficial statistics based on hair and eyes, Mrs. John F. Kennedy would never recognize our description of her late husband any more than your mother could guess whom you meant by your character sketch of her sister. We are strangers conversing in the dark of ignorance and unconscious discrimination.

We fail to make friends by falling victim to our first impression; before we know it we judge innocent bystanders by association with someone we used to know who wore her hair like that, or who went to the same school. Our new acquaintance keeps turning into the person he reminds us of. Rather than starting this new relationship from scratch, we find we are quickly engaged in old feuds, grinding axes relevant to another situation. Instead of distinguishing an individual we may be choosing sides, collecting supporters or antagonists, busily cataloguing this newcomer so we can have a familiar target.

We don't care who he is; we care about the recitation of the memory verse that matches the tribe to which we tag him. Depending on whether he is a liberal or fundamentalist, Negro or white, capitalist or socialist, whether he is higher up the ladder, old or young, we whip out the "set" speech we have well-worn and ready. We shall probably never really meet the one and only man like this before us. We are moving in on our straw man, and he must further conceal himself behind his defense mechanisms and ego props. "My family background is Nob Hill. . . ." "My cousin who works in the Pentagon. . . ." The exchange is not live, but cut-and-dried as soon as we have pinned each other down.

"Aha, so you are a Frenchman." ("I know what Frenchmen are like.") "So you are a preacher." (Immediately we jump to conclusions about this preacher from the image we carry on file. Preachers have barrels of dismal sermons, drink tea, and are not nearly as bright as the top of the class who went into medicine or banking.) We keep the interview safely static. We tend to petrify people into that initial place, completely forgetting that a person is no post but "a bird in flight." It is natural and common for men to impose opinions upon one another rather than to draw one another out. How often have you and I coaxed another out of his shell and into confidence and courage to be himself?

Usually we are moving so fast today, and are so shackled with shyness, insecurity, or unconscious prejudice, much of what we think we see in another is only the reflection in our lens. We magnify what we're looking for. How can bundles of brittle nerves, brimming over with leftover reactions, see straight into another's eyes, to say nothing of understanding? A scoundrel expects chicanery, a suspicious nature suspects more than the situation warrants. The ugly duckling's comments about the May Queen may be slanted. Jones may be a yes man simply because he has no choice in my dogmatic company. Neither the dropout nor the Phi Beta Kappa can be unbiased about their alma mater or the teacher most loved or detested. The bad-tempered may be scouring society for bad tempers to excuse their own, for misery of any kind loves company; gossipers or failures will hunt for fellow sufferers. Our observations of one another are stained and pressed with our projections. We may not be going through an introduction to someone but experiencing a side reaction.

The man and wife glaring at each other across the table of court proceedings do not know each other any better than when as bride and groom they gazed into eyes made nearsighted by cloud nine. And how many couples live together legally whose real relationship crystallized long ago at some level of cold war? She nags at him, and he retaliates in procrastination in a sterile vicious circle. There is no meeting of minds at all. They think they know each other, but they know only one side of the knot of twisted emotions that they have allowed to entangle them. They are not deepening a friendship, but are in the habit of assuming fixed battle positions. He barricades himself incommunicado behind his briefcase or the paper, she counterattacks with a chronic tardiness or by marrying into many women's organizations. They have never honestly revealed themselves to each other for fear of ridicule or judgment. They cannot share their sufferings and dare not risk their most precious thoughts in such an uninviting climate. These two may be celebrating their fiftieth wedding anniversary, yet have never really wed. They are strangers to the

death, ostracizing each other from the sweet lifeline of communion.

Who am I? The face my friend or enemy shows me, or the
heart he withholds or gives to me, is so much at my mercy. Let
us all then, before we plunge headlong into the mystery of
life's reception line, begin our introductions deliberately with
self.

"Know thyself." No one does, yet everyone must if he is
ever to gain consciousness. It is easier to hide in the indistinguishable crowd, but to become alive is to wake up with a start
of recognition. We might as well be buried anonymously as
unknown soldiers as to have no more proof of our identity
than our passport picture and transcript of credits. Who am I
really? Only a temporary clod of conditioned reflexes? A
grease spot in the making? Man, woman, thing of evil? Child?
Whose child? Anything special worth noting? Define me from
everyone else.

You and I are not meant to live and die a cog in a system of
education, nor streamlined as an automated beast of burden.
We are to be men. Before we abdicate this honor or have it
snatched from us; before we thicken the plot further with the
sicknesses of our own emotional conflicts, let us first each be
man enough to make friends with himself.

Who am I? I am not who I would like others to think I am. I
don't want to be seen before breakfast without cosmetics or in
unretouched photographs. The minister does not care to have
his chief deacon calling on him while he is weathering a
domestic crisis. It is embarrassing to have the boss catch me
borrowing money at the bank again or to have friends in-
formed of courses I flunked in school. I prefer to be photo-
graphed in my Sunday best, so advantageously that not even
my best friends would be able to recognize me, any more than
they would recognize me from my own autobiography.

I am not who I think I am. I suffer from delusions of

grandeur along with you. "Wait till you hear my side of the story." I probably select my friends because they share this prejudice in my favor—so far as I know. I may not be so sick as to think myself Napoleon, but I am no doubt busy giving myself the benefit of the doubt. I am a totally different person with different people. With one I am an introvert, with another I can clown. Which one is more like me?

Before you read on, jot down three facts that would identify you. One young woman put down: (1) journalist, (2) daughter of Robert Underwood, (3) fiancée of Henry J. Moore. How favored would you feel if you were Henry J. Moore, stuck in third place? Does listing the profession first betray that this young woman is chiefly interested in her profession? Do you gain any insight on your list of unconscious priorities? What glaring omissions did you make? Put down the first word that pops into your head, then the next, and the next. Repeat the game tomorrow night to see if you notice any trends in words. Doing this rapidly without forethought is one way of cracking the door to your deeper mind. There is more to each of us than we are conscious of. The larger part of us, like the larger portion of the iceberg, is below the surface, the subconscious and the unconscious. All this is I, too, explored and annexed or not.

Pure Freud is now passé, but he unlocked the door on our unconscious, and opened a new era in self-understanding. He discovered that this unappreciated domain was not an attic stored with dead wood, but a furnace of highly flammable material. Just because we are unconscious of memories doesn't mean they are not influential. Much of our behavior is being determined in those secret chambers of this dynamic territory, to which we are introduced in dreams.

Here are some indications of the activity of the unconscious. We tend, for instance, to find our own faults in others, completely unconscious of the reason. The elder brother in Jesus' parable, for instance, without any facts, jumped to the conclusion that the prodigal son had spent his money on harlots. How did he know? Harlots came into the picture from the back of the elder brother's mind. Much of us is repressed into our unconscious minds—for instance, our fear. We prefer to think, naturally, that we are not yellow. So one self-appointed hero rode to the operating table scoffing at his family's tremors: "It's me for the slab today." So far as he or anyone else could tell, he didn't know what fear was. But underneath the anesthesia he screamed some other things to show quite plainly that he was approaching panic but had repressed it all out of his conscious thought. What did you say under the pentothal? While dreams and deliriums need interpretation, since they speak in symbols and in parables, they are not at all irrelevant, but make sense. They represent the "you" that you haven't or won't acknowledge. Freud referred to the dream as "the royal road to the unconscious."

You may even have nightmares. They are not just bits of undigested beef but puzzling revelations. A man in mental illness is stuck in a perpetual nightmare, and most sane men have these occasional nocturnal seizures. One of C. G. Jung's patients labored under such terrible mental strain he couldn't trace the cause. Something so overwhelming was eating him he could not bear to think of it, so he locked it out of his mind. But repressing it didn't get rid of it; the problem continued its clamor below, bombarding him in dreams and in a general state of dread more difficult because unidentified.

Every night he dreamed he walked by a boiling sea. At a certain point a huge monster scurried out of the depths and came for him. Before he could move his legs it clutched him in its claws and carried him out and under till he awoke, sweating and screaming. Of course, there was actually no such monster, except in legends. There was not even a seashore nearby. But that man's business and family life, his entire fortune and reputation, were in extreme peril—life was closing in. He couldn't face all the impending horror in the cold light of day, so his mind was going into emergency session at night, signaling S.O.S. in symbolic dream language. The sea and the monster dramatized the facts of life he could neither admit nor articulate till he found a steady enough friendship to enable him to cough the repression into safer consciousness. There is no such thing as a dream that has no meaning.

A slip of the lip is not accidental, but perhaps lifting the lid of our unconscious. J. P. Morgan was very sensitive about his immense nose, so it was not accidental when one flustered hostess quavered, "Mr. Morgan, do you take nose in your tea?" A minister once introduced me as the author of *The Parables He "Sold,"* which may have betrayed more unconscious monetary interest than he was prepared to admit. Another minister almost gave himself away when in a high church wedding he invoked in a powerfully solemn voice: "Let us play—er, pray." Freud writes: "A young woman who is the dominating spirit of her house, said of an ailing husband, that he had consulted the doctor about a wholesome diet for himself, and then added, 'The doctor said that diet has nothing to do with his ailments, and that he can eat and drink what *I* want.' "[1] Freud told of Mrs. Walter D. Lamar, a speaker addressing the Georgia Division of the United Daughters of the Confederacy, who closed with the words:

> Let the world know the wisdom, the kindness, the justice of the great and only President of the Confederate States of America—Abraham Lincoln. . . .

"It was just one of those slips that may happen at moments of enthusiasm," Mrs. Lamar said. "Yes! The speaker is right,"

Freud goes on, "but we must know that the process of enthusiasm is nothing but a heightened emotional state in which conscious attention is almost completely suspended. In such a state, one unwittingly displays his true feelings and as under the influence of alcohol, the truth comes out."[2]

Leaving your purse on someone's sofa might reveal your wish to return. Without giving it any thought you just happen to sit down where you prefer. Freud was candid enough to confess, "Of a great number of professional calls, I only forgot those that I was to make on patients whom I treated gratis or on colleagues."[3] Forgetting your wife's birthday may be giving yourself away. What would the groom think of the bride who forgot to come to her wedding? What we are prompted to remember or forget, the joke that happens to come to mind, and on whom it is told, expose feelings we try to conceal from ourselves. Your sudden laughter when your bishop collapses in a heap on the ice may confess more delight than humor. Your wife may not take it lightly if you wake up cooing an old girl friend's name.

One psychiatrist humorously diagnoses his patients by their punctuality in keeping appointments. If the patient is ahead of time, he is a case of anxiety; if he is precisely on time, he is a compulsive; and if he is late, resentful. While this is an oversimplification, our mannerisms or reactions are spelling out unconscious aspects of our personality. Our negative attitude toward all authority figures may reveal resentment against the impact of parents still dominating our lives.

This volume hopes to help you trace your origin and taste your destiny, not in general, but in particular. We have in mind more than statistics; we mean an unveiling of your deepest soul, at least to you and God. The fresh insights of psychology joined with our faith equip us for a new excitement of self-consciousness.

Where do I look for me? Let us embark upon that adventurous rendezvous with the assistance of science, but not without God's, hoping in the end to achieve that delicate balance of humility and self-confidence captured in prayer by a slave:

> O Lord,
> I ain't what I oughta be;
> I ain't what I wanta be;
> I ain't what I'm gwina be.
> But thanks, Lord,
> I ain't what I used to be.
> Amen.

2
WHO WAS I?

H ow can we arrange for you to meet your old self? It is still undecided whether it is good to be psychoanalyzed, but we begin with the discovery of that science and where one goes from there to distinguish himself from among the disintegrating slivers. In the strangest, yet simplest way, our identity is concealed in our childhood. T. S. Eliot's moving line in *Four Quartets* takes us back to that world which Freud recovers for us: "In my beginning is my end."

Sigmund Freud conceded the origin of psychoanalysis to his colleague, Dr. Joseph Brewer, a prominent general practitioner, who accidently stumbled into it.

The patient concerned was a young girl of unusual education and talent, who had become ill while nursing her father to whom she was very much attached. Dr. Brewer states that when he took her as a patient, she presented a variegated picture of paralyses with contractures, inhibitions, and states of psychic confusion. Through an accidental observation Brewer discovered that the patient could be freed from such disturbances of consciousness if she could be enabled to give verbal expression to the affective phantasies which dominated her. Brewer elaborated this experience into a method of treatment. He hypnotized her and urged her to tell him what oppressed her at the time, and by this simple method he freed her from all her symptoms. The significance of the case lay in this fact, that in her waking state the patient knew nothing about the origin of her symptoms, but once hypnotized, she immediately knew the connection between her symptoms and some of her past experiences. All her symptoms were traceable to experiences during the time when she had nursed her sick father. Moreover, the symptoms were not arbitrary and senseless but could be traced to definite experiences and forgotten reminiscences of that emotional situation.[1]

Psychoanalysis has undergone many refinements since this historic first case, not always measuring up to the genius of Freud, who was in every way its founder despite Brewer's initial discovery.

Freud soon forsook hypnotism for suggestion. By encouraging the patient to associate freely whatever entered his mind, Freud found that the door of the subconscious would open about as readily as under hypnosis and to much better effect. Nothing the patient volunteered was ever irrelevant, but would join the caravan of thoughts winding back to specific experiences the patient had been unable to bear in consciousness and had repressed too deeply to recall without help. Once these emotional disturbances were reproduced and put into words and tears, they were then powerless to secrete anxiety or psychosomatic symptoms.

Across the Christian years, the quiet priest or minister true to his calling has been a patient and unpublicized witness to substantially this same process of psychotherapy. Although it was certainly necessary for Freud to sharpen and introduce the method in modern terms, our finest students of the soul, from Augustine to Tillich, have found, as Kierkegaard has written, that our most difficult experiences "make a man dumb in order to keep him in their power,"[2] and we find freedom only through their expression.

A woman comes to such a doctor or minister practically paralyzed with fright and inferiority. Perhaps she has a physical symptom for which repeated diagnosis has found no organic cause. Probably she has been referred in desperation by another physician. Maybe she is like the woman to whom the physician Luke referred who had spent her means and her years on doctors and grown worse. Now her rest is ruined with nightmares and her days with dread, and she resorts to religion. Or she may have flitted about the church altar fussing with flowers, beating her wings like a moth against the light's exterior, unconsciously yearning for a sufficiently adequate confessional that could pick its painful way back through the labyrinth of her life to the needling source of her despair.

Freud poetically refers to any hysterical symptom as the "monument which the problem threw up at its origin," such as a compulsion to flee, being unable to sit still very long, or obesity. But the identifying inscription on this puzzling monument has been lost and the process by which the mystery is unearthed and resolved is, to use Freud's powerful images, like excavating the ruins of a buried city. The confessor at the altar, whose quiet understanding quickens the communicant's confidence, is familiar with the process of psychoanalysis.

The patient must be absolutely free to begin any way he cares. He must have permission to be insulting and illogical without the threat of a counselor's defensiveness. Often he will start the interview, "I don't know why I ever came to *you*," or, "You must think me stupid," or, "There's nothing wrong, really." Perhaps he refers to a minor last-minute domestic crisis, or tries out other secondary cares on this strange new confidant to test his tolerance, although he has selected the most approachable and reliable person the pressure of his need permits.

Time and again, I have found that if the counselor is equal to his requirements, often in the first few seconds, even contrary to the patient's intentions, the conversation will be out of his control. He will have plunged into the past, blurting out, in fact, flooding the conference room with long-repressed and emotionally charged memories. The sufferer is full of consternation at the speech of this irresponsible stranger inside himself.

The feelings and thoughts so rapidly making their exodus come forth as fertile as when they were repelled in childhood. They were too difficult for the victim to handle consciously back then, so, as Freud has explained, they were thrown out of the mind much as disturbers of the peace are tossed out of a meeting. But just as with a meeting, these recalcitrants continue their clamor outside until they finally are readmitted and consciously assimilated into the assembly of our thoughts. Until this ultimate peace is made with these unbearable memories, they will continue their criminal activity under the surface, producing anxiety, depression, or physical illness.

It is not enough for the patient simply to report the facts of that heartbreak; his heart must break a little bit again. He must be so immersed in his sad tale that he not only recalls, but recries the tears—this alone discharges their sting. Coughing up traumas is like childbirth or vomiting. The patient anticipates the experience with mixed feelings of reluctance and eagerness. The creative interviews are those when the patient cannot bear to keep the appointment and cannot bear not to. Psychotherapy is like a long-drawn-out operation which the patient both longs for and dreads, but he must undergo this operation without the benefit of anesthesia. Throughout the series of interviews he will feel the surgeon's knife as it opens and cleanses the wounds that could never heal, despite the superficial skin grafts and Band-Aids of renewed effort. The patient suffers through his catharsis, working through the bygone gloom and terror, this time with his counselor's help, where before he had been stopped and downed alone.

Freud called this process "abreaction," rightly feeling that it was mandatory for the patient's present and future health to go back and react to childhood events to which he was too fearful or inadequate to react properly at that time. "A sentence of general pathology says that every process of development brings with it the germ of pathological dispositions in so far as it may be inhibited, delayed, or incompletely carried out."[3]

Life will not allow us to get away without living our experiences simply because they are too much for us at the time. If we sidestep a sorrow, for instance, refusing to make the down payment of emotion it demands from us, we must later make up for it at interest. I know of one dreadful Christmas morning when a little boy raced downstairs to devour his long-anticipated stocking, only to discover it contained coal as punishment for being a bad boy. His desolation was so extensive he was unable even to whisper anything in response to so thorough a rejection. That was so high a wall of experience, along with other similar rejections, he never made it over; it stuck in him, mute and buried, like a large piece of festering shrapnel, furnishing for years unexplainable negative feelings and behavior. This will continue until he finds the attachment and rapport with a surrogate father which will ventilate that and other outrageous robberies.

Or a woman in her forties who came to see me, struggling with suffocating feelings of destructiveness, finally recalls an attempted suicide in her teens and the life of panic and rejection that led up to it. She had tried, unsuccessfully, to live oblivious to these feelings. Her mother was one of those people who patted her on the head, murmuring "sweet nothings," but underneath and lurking in her eyes the child saw that her mother hoped she would disappear.

One sufferer at last remembered "dying a thousand deaths" sensing the rupture of violence when her father kicked the

puppy down the dark basement stairs. Or again he stood mon-
sterlike and threatening in her doorway, forcing her against
her will to say her prayers. This "imposed-upon" child was
never permitted even to stamp her foot in anger. So now,
during the days of her therapy, when she returns to do justice
to those experiences thrust upon her before her guard was up,
she finds herself going about the house yielding to a strong
returning desire to stamp her foot.

Another young woman gravitates in a rush of tears to the
time when she was four, and her five-year-old sister forced her
to lose every game they played even when she won, pinning
her arms while the necessary points were piled up.

A grown man remembers with trembling lip the beginning
of this sense of utter worthlessness as though it had happened
that afternoon. The incident was in high school, where the
coach publicly dismissed (or was it denounced?) him from
the basketball tryouts with the brutal words, "Son, you'd better stick to your flute."

These painful secrets were resurrected in the same climate of
desolation as in their original burial. And often, almost simultaneously, physical symptoms owing their origin to these submerged icebergs melted away upon expression. As Freud put
it, "You may regard the psycho-analytic treatment only as a
continued education for the overcoming of childhood rem-
nants."[4]

This process of "chimney sweeping," of self-discovery, must
continue until completed. Each of us is mysterious and unique,
but what ails us are these specific instances, stinging us like
splinters until pinpointed and articulated. Advice and encouragement to be cheerful are most aggravating to someone whose
disposition is seeping with such a grievance. The difficulty will
not be dislodged, it must be disarmed. The conference room
must offer the atmosphere of a poultice drawing out the sting.

The hurt one must not be told off but heard out—to his heart's content.

It won't do for the sufferer simply to see and speak with someone. He requires for his remedy the establishment of a steady relationship. To be effective, the relationship must offer far more elbow room and much less pressure than the long line at the usual confessional permits. It must be much more personal and complimentary than the squeeze of moments dropped as crumbs by any therapist who is spread too thin to really take anyone in.

In the process of discovering who one is arises the experience of transference. We begin again with Freud, but acknowledge that the necessary correction and conclusion of this matter rests with such men as Buber and Tournier and ultimately with Christ.

> There occurs . . . the so called phenomenon of *transference* (ubertragung), that is, he (the patient) applies to the person of the physician a great amount of tender emotion, often mixed with enmity, which has no foundation in any real relation, and must be derived in every respect from the old wish fantasies of the patient, which can no longer be called back into memory, is accordingly lived over by the patient in his relations to the physician, and only by such a living over of them in the *transfer* is he convinced of the existence and the power of these unconscious sexual excitations. The symptoms . . . are the precipitates of earlier love experiences . . . [and] can only be dissolved in the highest temperature of the experience or transfer and transformed into other psychic products. . . . You must not think that the phenomenon of transfer, about which I can unfortunately say too little here, is created by the influence of the psychoanalytic treatment. The transfer arises spontaneously in all human relations . . . and it is the special bearer of therapeutic influences.[5]

The technique and professional ingenuity of the psychoanalyst or confessor, important as they are, are not so important as the science of psychotherapy insists. More significant is the personality of the psychotherapist and the quality of the rapport which limits or extends the depth of the transfer. This is more important than can possibly be imagined.

Freud emphasized this aspect of psychotherapy by commenting,

> "I say it is hardly avoidable that the personal relation to the physician should not become unduly prominent, at least for some time. Indeed, it seems as if such an influence exerted by the physician is a condition under which alone a solution of the problem is possible."[6]

Yet this does not underline the matter strongly enough, for the patient is not only suffering from reminiscences, but at the same time from sick or missing relationships. Buber shouts, "A soul is never sick alone, but always through a betweenness, a situation between it and another existing being."[7] He is suffering from a starvation diet of love, and has lived perhaps up until this relationship without ever having enjoyed a stable friendship. These interviews probably represent the nearest thing to a father's attention he has ever known. The communication of previously locked-up complaints is a necessary corollary, but only a corollary to the supreme luxury of the long-denied (symbolic) parental lap that has at last arrived, dignified and formal though it may be. The therapeutic effect of the confessor is proportionate to how much more receptive he is than a mere microphone or than someone who is simply paid to pay attention and be permissive. The patient's wound calls not simply for the doctor's clinical tools, but the doctor himself.

Each of us must find this experience, as Kierkegaard says, with a surrogate father if not from our parent. "I learnt from him the meaning of fatherly love and so was given some idea of divine fatherly love, the one unshakeable thing in life, the true archimedean point."[8]

Keeping the conference room quiet will not in itself loosen the sufferer's tongue. The revelation requires communion, and the unwinding of the snarled skein proceeds according to the capacity of the psychotherapist to be human. Freud's humility and honesty played a far greater role in his therapy than he ever realized.[9] He so often credited his *method* for the results that came because of the man he was. Many who have mastered Freud's techniques have never conducted a creative interview because they lacked his immense personal charm and magnanimity—his extraordinary capacity to inspire confidence. These personal qualities were more responsible than any prescription for causing a patient to come to catharsis.

Beyond this, so much depends on the patient's capacity to appreciate his confessor. His confidence in his counselor is of even greater significance than the counselor's merit. Time after time I have seen this principle in operation. Those whose confidence in me was restricted—those, for instance, who came because they couldn't afford or were too afraid to go elsewhere—were never greatly helped. But those whose confidence in me for some reason knew no bounds were helped so far beyond and aside from any power I possessed that I recognized over and over that it was not at all false modesty that made Jesus explain to those who attributed their cure to him: "Go in peace; *your faith* has made you well."

We must not be afraid to confess the effect of these relationships on the confessor or the analyst. It is sheer folly to suppose he is an insulated bystander to the gamut of emotions alternately freezing and burning his companion in the conference room. Even the most self-contained counselor, for all his poker face, cannot resist at least inward responses to the shock treatments administered by his "foster children." Inevitably, the most callous referee is absorbing bits of their recollected beating. Only a dead man could be indifferent to this unabating storm of inner fury and intense affection directed at him. He may conceal it, but he is not immune. Any adjustment or transformation in his client's life causes a corresponding one in the counselor's. Unless the physician is treating his patient as an "it," there is an intense, though unverbalized, dialogue rioting between them.

Buber speaks of "inclusion"—experiencing the other side. He means, according to Weizsacker,

> that the doctor allows himself to be changed by the patients, that he allows all the impulses that proceed from the person of the patient to affect him, that he is receptive, not only with the objective sense of sight, but also with hearing, which brings the "I and Thou" more effectively together. Only through the ever-new insertion of his personality can the doctor bring his capacities to full realization in his relation with his patients.[10]

No doctor is impervious despite his most sedate bedside manner. He is only human. He may be sitting there with a headache, or with the last sharp words of his wife or his broker ringing in his ears. And all these feelings and frustrations are transparent to his perceptive patients, who of course also bask under his periods of tranquillity. The patient detects the subtlest shifts of mood in the counselor. "You are not listening to me today—you are far away." "You appear sad. Are you worried about anything?" I remember finally confiding to one client my plans for moving so he would not be surprised when they were announced publicly. He replied, "Oh, I have felt this for some time."

The counselor might relish an artificial one-way relationship. But life won't have it. Any time a therapist steps into the life of another, he exposes himself and becomes vulnerable. Otherwise, the patient is really rejected as a person of no consequence, and the doctor plays dead to the life offered him.

This is not to recommend that the therapist overwhelm the overloaded patient with the doctor's problems. He acknowledges to the patient that he, too, is a "fellow traveler to the grave'—avoiding the unspoken insinuation that he is safely above all the problems that engulf his charge. Unless such a give-and-take relationship exists, the client is crammed into the humiliating position of asking help of an automaton to whom he can be of no help in return—to whom the patient can never truly be a person. Such masquerading on the doctor's part paints a false picture. No machine can come to a patient's rescue. It comforts the client to discover that behind the desk is no graven image, but a fellow mortal "tempted in all points" even as he is.

The counselor's humility is as precious to the patient as the counselor's maturity—is there a distinction? St. Francis of Assisi insisted that the very reason the helpless found their way to his door was not his radiance, but his fellowship of wretchedness. "Nowhere," he said, "is there a more miserable sinner than I." Buber explains, "The abyss in the patient calls to the abyss, the real unprotected self, in the doctor, and not to his confidently functioning security of action."[11]

Ultimately, what matters most to a patient is whether or not in his interviews he is talking to a real man or a professional fragment. The patient is not after listening time but living room. The sufferer yearns to be *with someone*. As poet Paul Engle has written, "But in the human house of his presence I felt safe."[12] "Finally, it implies for both a laying aside of the preoccupation with professional analysis, diagnosis, and evaluation in favor of an acceptance and understanding of the client based on true attitudes of respect which are deeply and genuinely felt by the therapist."[13]

Buber's claim to greatness, as Trub has said, must surely be the ideal of anyone who dares to practice psychosynthesis. "He steps forth as this single man and talks directly to men."[14] Who was I? That shy occupant concealed in the recesses of our minds will unveil to that one who not only commands our highest confidence, but who responds to our transference with the highest form of friendship.

3
RESENTFUL?

"**H**E WAS ALWAYS such a sweet boy—so courteous. How could he commit this bloody massacre? His brother was the incorrigible one." Yet the "little gentleman" who endured the bullying with submissive smiles may commit psychopathic murder. Resentment is smoldering anger.

Just because he has never lost his temper or shown aggressiveness doesn't mean it isn't in him. It means, rather, that all of it is still in him, with no way out. The day came when the boy spoken of above went berserk with hostility. Having no valve to spill the lifelong accumulation of aggression, he overreacted. The potential killer may be the docile teacher's pet. But it is he, rather than the "bad" boy, who is filled to the brim with repressed rage.

Resentment may be caused in several ways. It unconsciously builds up in a boy whose mother pre-empts his life. She hovers over him unhealthfully close, denying him individuality and the right and privacy to make mistakes or do differently. He suffers into his teens from the intensive care of the incubator. She has anticipated his wishes, presumed to improve upon his private life, and predicted his thinking in such a way that he has been robbed of the right to jump to his own conclusions. If he so much as shows a mind of his own, she feels rebuffed and swiftly dissolves him to a manageable puddle by the tyranny of her imaginatively staged tears. He is no match for her ingenuity. Her encroachment slowly removes his spine, for he doesn't dare exercise his contrary opinion. His developing dreams, breathing murder against her interference, leave him so conscience-stricken that it even lowers his resistance to her continued monopoly of his life and thought. There is no way out. He is arrested as a homosexual, or as the victim of anxiety steaming from hate, or both.

Therapists speak of such an emotionally smothered lad sitting across from a counselor's desk doodling monster pictures of his father or mother. The psychotherapist rightly encourages him to continue to ventilate these buried grudges there. Little egos that have been overpowered must have this opportunity finally to have their say about this unsatisfactory state of their emotional affairs. The physician is not encouraging disobedience, but rather permitting the boy to defend himself against a totalitarian regime in which he suffered from having to buckle under—and in which obedience meant obliteration. The boy was not simply made to mind, he had been taken over, treated as though he were a thing with no side nor ground to stand on. He was not won—he was callously overrun.

No one has ever *heard* this boy or let him *be*. He has no ear into which to pour the story of his misuse. The walls around some persons are too high—seemingly self-sufficient and enclosed. The contrary is true of this child. Possessive adults have prevented him from erecting any kind of protective fence about himself. He has been brainwashed from the beginning. He has not been allowed to control any area of his life. He has no place he could call his own. Perhaps parents rummage through his room without permission, intrude upon his bath without knocking. His brothers take over his toys according to their wishes, without his ever having the blessed prerogative of being consulted on anything. He knows no life of his own. He is being stepped on, and he resents it. Unless someone soon hears him out and helps him rectify this intolerable condition, he too may erupt in violence.

That boy becomes a man. When someone comes to visit him, he feels trapped until they decide to leave. The tragedy for him, in this as in similar instances, is that he is not in control of the situation. These guests decide the duration of their stay. He is at the mercy of whoever comes along. This must not go on. His mental health here depends upon his learning how to terminate the visit himself. Not until he has demonstrated and enjoyed the honor of playing genuine host to his complete satisfaction will he be safe. In the meantime, gruffness would be superior to his continued groveling. A counselor can encourage him to experiment with his own solutions before the increasing pressure blasts him apart.

Long ago, in my early ministry, the phone rang late one night. I awakened to a voice reduced to a whisper by fear, "I don't know why I called you." The words were squeezed out in short bursts. I could tell that it was only with the greatest effort that this person could communicate at all. I was dealing with someone in the gravest state of panic. Finally, she blurted out that there was a bottle of sleeping pills waiting to be taken beside her bed. Her nights had gradually grown stiff with terror until she could neither bear to close her eyes from fear, nor keep them open from fatigue. Now she was cornered and had just faltered in the act of taking her own life, not because of the threat of oblivion, but because she was suddenly seized with the thought that suicide might not bring oblivion.

After many long midnight calls, she at last surrendered her name. She was of another faith. I gathered from her conversation that she had graduated from a European university with a degree in Ancient History. I insisted that I allow me to refer her to a psychiatrist, and quickly realized my mistake. Her slim margin of security had been exhausted in establishing this contact with me. It alarmed her that I apparently felt she was in too critical a condition for my assistance. She had already been to many doctors and would be referred no further; "I cannot bear to go into this again with anyone else." At last her confidence developed enough that she could attempt her first face-to-face conference with me. She was fifteen minutes late; then the phone rang. She had called to make sure I had not forgotten. "Where are you?" I asked. "In a booth across the street."

She was blond, very beautiful, and overweight. Those first interviews were crammed with the most painful silences. "These lights are like those of a police station." "Please say something. This silence is choking me." Only by the close of the interview was she even able to explain her inability to speak. "I want to tell you so much, I can't get anything out. Everything wants to come at once, so nothing can come." The doorway of her confession was clogged with memories clamoring for exit.

Her father and mother had died recently, and she was appalled to find that their departure was relief. Behind her fear was loneliness, behind that, guilt, then weakness, and lurking back of it all lay fury.

The hours in conference before she found her tongue were long, but too charged with her fright to be boring. I despaired of her ever being able to tell me her anguish. At last I suggested that if she could not speak perhaps she could write something down and bring it with her. The next time she handed me this:

Nightmare

I am alone on a barren windswept crag. As far as my eyes can see there is nothing but desolation and emptiness. Raging waves beat a mad tattoo against the jagged rocks below as with a horrendous crash the sea thrusts forth her thundering agents of destruction.

In the grey heavens above a solitary gull flits mournfully across the vast unending emptiness of space. I am filled with such a feeling of utter loneliness and melancholy as makes me weep at the sight of this, the last living thing I shall ever see.

Long dormant flecks of memory thrust their pointed shafts into my consciousness as I seem to recall a day long years ago when I first dwelt upon the terrifying feelings of unreality that had engulfed my life. But I know now in these last fleeting moments that we are all of us living in an unreal world, tormented by the memory of things we have done and haunted by the things we have not dared to do.

I am suddenly become aware of a crashing silence such as I have never known. In the blessed peace of the titanic stillness the awesome fear relinquishes its vise-like grip upon my senses and as the shadows around me deepen into a fading twilight I thrill in soaring ecstasy to the phantasmic figure that approaches me now from beyond the horizons of another world. . . .

She would sit by the hour hunched in her chair, sunk hypnotically in her secret world of terror. I feared it must soon get the best of her unless she could admit me. At last she began: "I awakened with a nightmare. I have never been so terrified. I couldn't even get my breath. Finally I got the window open." "Would you care to tell me about it?" ". . . I can't remember it. I won't. I won't." Her face was contorted, her hands clutching the chair tight. Then she tried to tell me something. I couldn't hear and I asked her to repeat it. She moistened her lips and tried again. This time it was barely audible.

"I have had this dream often, but not so awful." Each sentence was an achievement that left her panting. The words for her were as rough to coin as retching. "I am alone in a dark house. It has endless corridors and rooms. . . . Two huge cats are fighting, clawing. . . . Their screeching is horrendous." She spat each word as though it were repugnant. "I try in vain to separate them and throw them out, but they are back at it in another room. Oh, it is too dreadful to think of any longer." She held her ears. "I can't remember any more. . . . I want to run away . . . but I can't move."

I waited, and in that heavily charged silence thought a prayer. "Tell me now what you are thinking." "Nothing. My mind's a blank. I don't know why I came to see you." Then she lapsed into her reverie again, reliving the life she led as a child in that haunted house. At last she whispered hoarsely: "My mother and father used to fight incessantly. They would scream at each other even after I had gone to bed, following each other from room to room. I could not bear it; I died. The noise and their fierceness was suffocating . . . once they were shrieking at each other across the dinner table. Suddenly my father rose and ripped his shirt and coat down the back. I was numb." She was so shaken and exhausted after this and other ordeals of talk that I often had to let her use another conference room to recover sufficient poise and strength to leave. Always for her, the dream was "the royal road to the unconscious," as Freud insisted. It was as though it were a distraction for me to insert leading questions. If I let her alone, the meaning of the dream would come to her immediately, as though reporting the dream prompted the memory of the experience it represented.

She was a child of trauma. Hours of speechlessness often succeeded the voluble ones. Yet the most productive interviews would begin in deep discouragement: "I can't talk to you anymore." "Tell me your dream." "I can't remember it." Then the dream would come. After that I would finally request, "Why not tell me what comes to mind?" Often in the next sentence after she had said, "I don't know what the dream means," the memory of the experience would return. "I remember stealing as a child. I took several boxes of pencils from the ten-cent store and gave one to the other third-graders to make friends. One day the store manager came into our school room to speak to us. . . . He said my name. . . . I was shattered. . . . He made everyone give back their pencils. I was obliterated. . . . They called my father. He had to go down to the court. I begged and begged him not to tell my mother. He promised. . . . Soon after that, I was sitting beside my mother while she was sewing. I was counting the buttons on her dress; they went all the way down to the hem. Then she took my hand and went: 'Rich man, poor man, beggarman, THIEF,' screaming and thrashing about hysterically when she came to that word, and when I began to sob uncontrollably she shut me up and lectured me."

Layer after layer of recollections she had consciously forgotten was born again. Frequently, she would begin in a cold sweat. One time: "I awakened this morning at the point of suffocation. I cannot bear another such night." "What was your dream?" ". . . I can't remember a thing . . . There was a blinding light . . . I am in the front seat of a car. I am about five years old . . . There has just been a terrible accident. The other car is upside down, burning furiously. I think, yes, there are people still inside. Oh, that light. Oh, no, no, no. They never told me . . . How could they do that to me? Oh, it was all *my* fault. They always said it was the other driver's, but . . . yes, I jumped in my father's way while he was driving . . . My mother lost the son she doted on, my father was in the hospital for months. . . ."

She had arrived at the most excruciating of her repressions.

The source of her resentment lay in the insidious way her parents had deprived her of the facts. In a superficial way they led her to believe she was not to blame, but in their undercurrent of feelings, she was made to feel in thousands of depreciating looks the full responsibility for the misfortunes that had fallen on the family. Without doing it directly, her father and mother persecuted and tortured her as the scapegoat for their unhappiness. She could tell only too well that she was an untouchable. She looked on herself with horror and loathing, but deep down she resented such unfairness fiercely. For as long as she could remember she was subtly taught that there was something so wrong with her that it was unmentionable. Once she had begged her father, while scraping the ground, clinging to the cuff of his trousers, to forgive her for something she had done to him so terrible he had never told her what it was, but he shook her off swearing: "Get the hell out of here."

As the therapy progressed, overwhelming rushes of rage would engulf her, making her afraid she might murder the next minor offender. Her kleptomania too had been in retaliation against a life minus parental affection. Handling such a barnful of deeply submerged aggression took practice and delicate befriending.

She nursed her father night and day during his last illness. The guilt she felt for hating him glued her to his hospital room. She drove herself relentlessly in his service; still she was not able to outmaneuver the pent-up murder in her heart. A stroke had struck him dumb, but he followed her everywhere with his eyes, mutely, piteously, begging pardon. He wanted only her to change his bandages, and once with the scissors in her hands, it was all she could do to restrain herself from using them to discharge her resentment. But his terrible suffering disarmed her memory, and after his funeral, in conference, she remembered the injury in childhood that had further angered them against each other. It welled up bitterly into words and stormed from her in screams of anguish and disgust. And when the corpse of this grievance had been exhumed, she found herself sobbing in sorrow for her terrible feelings against him. Once the fury had been fully stated, she discovered she could honestly accept her own imperfections and found forgiveness spontaneously. It is a Christian exercise in grace among friends. First came the resurrection of that smoldering resentment; then this freed the other devils it held prisoner.

Ultimately, the resolution of this damage of a lifetime was found in her genuine forgiveness of those who had wronged her, which came in its own good time. And no therapy is worth its salt short of that essential medicine.

A brilliant teen-age girl was referred to me suffering from nervousness and periodic tremors which she called "fits of the shakes." She began to confide childhood heartbreaks. Then one day, her knuckles white, tears scalding her cheeks, she began to hiss through clenched teeth her stomachful of antipathy against her father. He was her mother's mouse, meekly turning over every pay check, abdicating all dignity as man of the house, nightly descending the cellar stairs to abdicate as father of this girl in favor of his beer and stamps. She detested this image of "a basement man" and relived in the conference room the buried grievances she had garnered against him.

The day came when the last dregs of this hostility had surfaced, and she was clinically unburdened. But she kept coming back, as though she were waiting for some further word from me. At hand was a short story of a son who had forgiven his prodigal father. She invited me to read it aloud—until she sobbed her forgiveness of him. I saw her a few months later. The tremors had not returned, and the once pinched and worried face was filled with beauty. As we stood there, her eyes filled with the tears of that rarest and most mature of all the states of man's emotions. She took my hands in thanksgiving, which I realize was directed through me to God. I do not believe anyone can ever make a lasting peace with himself nor life until he makes his peace with God. What is confession for if not the thirst for absolution? And forgiveness is never an end in itself; inevitably it yields the floor to its superior, gratitude.

Ernest Gordon reported the paranoiac hatred that enveloped the allied prisoners at Chungai[1] for the cruelty and starvation to which they were subjected. He and his fellow prisoners were actually being consumed by the cancer of their animosity. They were not unaware of their disease, but they were nonetheless its helpless victims. Their days and nights were livid with the luxury of this rampant evil, and nothing good could come until forgiveness came to cultivate the ground of their hard feelings.

Recognition that one's resentment is focused on his mother-in-law may dismiss the migraine, but that does not *enable* him to escape the engulfing embrace of resentment. Relief and anything that could remotely resemble recovery must wait for reconciliation. The only medicine strong enough to banish hatred is forgiveness and love. Gordon identified that red-letter day when the necessary new spirit swept the prisoner-of-war camp. A young noncom was leading the men in the Lord's Prayer only to find that his was the only voice repeating the words, "Forgive us our trespasses as we forgive those who trespass against us." He started over the prayer again and this time hundreds joined in, sobbing. It was not only their salvation, but their recovery of health as well which was hanging on that one word, "Forgive."

No one is ever completely free of the return of the affliction of resentment, and the wise will seek a preventive. One vigorous octogenarian traced his happy longevity to his lifelong practice of praying first each night for the person who had treated him worst that day. "Praying for my enemies," he declared, "licked resentment before it lingered long enough to attack my digestion or interrupt my rest." No amount of insight or effort can outfight severe bouts of antagonism. The couch can alert us to the enemy, but the secret of triumph waits for us at the altar of God's forgiveness and in the grace that it alone confers.

4
GUILTY?

I N CONDUCTING our search for this unidentified person in us, we have discovered that the mildest-mannered man, as well as the aggressive one, may be bristling with hostility and dreaming revenge. We now continue the investigation into what amounts to a murder mystery; for the most angelic may be actually guiltiest. Hebrews shouldered their mistakes upon a scapegoat. Honesty here is harder to achieve.

A few victims are pathologically engulfed in guilt. They are so ill they prefer to think that they have committed the unpardonable sin—so they have resolved to enjoy an extremity of blame beyond even the hand of God to help. Neurotics multiply around us, morbidly preoccupied with what's wrong with them, luxuriating in this distinction they have won for themselves in evil. Lady Macbeth spent her madness rinsing her hands. One ex-convict introduces himself as "a cockroach in an exterminating company." You do not have to walk down the corridor of our mental hospitals very far before you meet a man who thinks he's Judas.

However, the average man pleads innocent. His brochure is impressive; his references can speak well of him without reservation. He is a soft white pillow, if not a marble pillar of the church; usually he at least makes a point of being seen at services once a month to indicate a discreet connection, but not naïve submission, to the church. He swears and tells off-color jokes just enough to prove he's one of the boys, and shakes his head in horror over those hoods in Harlem or the ignorant white trash smoldering in the South. He covets not the apostle's morals, but the banker's. His aim is to be in solid with the "in" group, to present the image of affluent respectability and indistinguishable decency, with nothing against him on his record. This man couldn't imagine being implicated in a crime and, if questioned, would answer in the pained innocence of a sixth-grader, "I didn't do anything. He did it." To him, sin is lawbreaking or not belonging to the Establishment or those outrageous disturbances he reads about in the paper. He has pronounced himself good, and his unspoken reproach to outsiders, underdogs, and those who get caught is simply, "Why can't you be like me?" His is a modern form of the disease of repressed guilt known to ancient times as Phariseeism.

Yet neither Holy Writ nor modern psychology could give this typical "success story" clearance. He is really the common example of the surreptitious grime of modern times. The minds most diseased with guilt are those unconscious of its existence. The men who killed Christ were not the last victims of its contagion. George Bernard Shaw insisted that he never would have touched the theme of the martyrdom of Joan of Arc had he not felt it was still a burning issue; that the same thing would take place today. The executive club may exact strict requirements for membership according to their clever slide rule, but this will not exclude the guilty. Guilt as virulent as in the days of the medieval torture chambers has put modern psychology in business. Salem burned innocent witches to assuage the public's unconscious guilt. And man today has never witch-hunted more assiduously. Fingers point always away from themselves. All the problems in the world are attributed to the obvious troublemakers such as the professor's wife, Martha, in *Who's Afraid of Virginia Woolf?* The noxious influence secreted by the literature on the newsstands presents an easy target.

The modern mind is quite resourceful in clearing its skirts, but even our more polished procedure is mainly disguised finger-pointing. The typical suburbanite has no idea of how much time he spends "seeking to justify himself." He absolves himself for his antichurch attitude by accusing his Victorian parents of forcing him to go to Sunday school. Hundreds of extenuating circumstances occur to us to excuse our tardiness or bad habits. We have no trouble explaining anything so we won't be left holding the bag.

Dr. Paul Tournier feels this personal refusal to bear responsibility to be the fundamental fomenter of war. The North and South still blame each other for the Civil War. "The drama of Europe," wrote André Malraux, "is the drama of a bad conscience." Mutual incrimination climbs from man to man, organizing into belligerent sides until it ignites in international bloodshed. According to Dr. Henri Baruk, "Guilt feelings hide behind hate campaigns."[1]

> Bring several people together and the first conflict will arise from wounded self-love, from the jealousy of the one over against the other, sometimes from the feeling of guilt. . . . Then the reactions of defense and justification begin to operate: the attempt is made to shift the discontent upon innocent victims, to ward off criticism and justified complaints by creating artificial culprits. The weakest are well designed to play this role of scapegoat. . . . The most atrocious civil wars, the crimes of fanaticism, and the wars of religion, or the ideological wars, are first fomented by agitators, by the entrepreneurs of hate, and only then do the base instincts of the masses explode.[2]

Modern men have further established their innocence by abolishing the word "sin" altogether. Our savants dismiss sin as a subnormal notion great-grandfather entertained. Sin to them is only a phantom that rattled the shutters of early Americana.

Can you imagine the chairman of the board of a great university bothering about it for a minute? Celia's confession in Eliot's *The Cocktail Party* describes the contemporary prejudice in which the pseudo-intelligentsia is caught:

> Well, my upbringing was pretty conventional—
> I had always been taught to disbelieve in sin.
> Oh, I don't mean that it was ever mentioned:
> But anything wrong from our point of view
> Was either bad form, or psychological.[3]

Making guilt inadmissable has made it all the more dangerous. Since it is undefined, sin now enjoys a reign of terror. We refuse to believe that there is anything to forgive. We will not recognize an occasion for a Redeemer. Shaw described this development by declaring that the "truly damned are those who are happy in hell."

The deadliest form of guilt orphaned from God is now abroad. Children suffer hopelessly from a disease that is incurable, for it has no diagnosis. Modern permissive parents inflict guilt on their youngsters in a way that would make Puritans and Victorians shudder. Instead of requiring goodness, children are expected to come across with special talents which their parents can display to friends—or they become a reproach. Boys and girls are tossed out on a sea of bitter competition without a good God to go to for assistance or for solace if they fail their god, success. Students are crushed by standards far more unattainable than commandments, and these ultimatums seem arbitrary, for they were originated at the caprice of convention or parental whims and not with the convincing backing of an Almighty God.

Failure used to be forgivable. Not now. This ambitious efficiency that determines our future now sends rejects straight to a hell worse by far than Jonathan Edwards ever knew.

Seldom is a child comforted these days with the thought that there is a heavenly Companion with him in his ups and downs. He is up against it on his own and "he'd better get down to business if he knows what is good for him." Parents may smile at his sensual sins, but he had better not be shy or unattractive. Nothing could be further from the mind of that failing school-boy today than that God still loves him dearly. One parent was told by a college admissions man that "there is no place for a 'late bloomer' here."

A junior in high school was flunking her math exam. Her parents simply could not tolerate anything less than college-preparatory grades, so she cheated and got caught. Consequently she attempted suicide, for she feared her parents would be equally incapable of accepting and forgiving her after that. She swore her confidant to secrecy about her attempt at suicide, for she felt they would not be able to forgive her for that either.

Guilt's tentacles spread out from childhood and headlock a man. Time itself will not simply neutralize this feeling. Guilt is a stone in the stomach, indigestible. A bad conscience has a memory like an elephant, paining a man with many of his most unforgettable experiences. The teacher who insisted he was a naughty child, the excessive righteous indignation shown him for staring at a nude picture the boys were passing around left him with the persisting notion that there was an indefinable ugliness fixed in him with which he was powerless to deal. Someone burned into a child's mind that he was a bad lot. Now he unconsciously strains to hear the creak on the stair of the suspicious parent trying to catch him.

A child's garden is stalked by guilt. And in common with all humanity he feels the guilt of the wrongs he actually did commit. Now that he is older, he only seems farther away from them. The blame bred into him the day mother caught him smoking behind the shed or stealing from her purse was magnified into the size of an international incident in his memory. The times he cheated in class or sports and did not get caught, the night he heard the cry for help and did nothing, or the day he spread the rumor that caused another's expulsion set his teeth on edge.

And here we are, stuck in this same pattern as adults, ingeniously rationalizing. We repress, but do not quite lay to rest, our misgivings about the dishonesty we feel necessary. Our perfectly good reasons for making out our income tax that way or for firing that employee somehow won't stand up, but return to plague us. We hate ourselves for pretending to like people we detest, for cowering on a committee instead of speaking out, for being unable to face a daughter after what she found out about us. There is the sickening activity in which one is inextricably involved down at the office which he could not recommend to his son. And what is preposterous, the best move we could possibly make now is invariably stained.

The Puritans gloried in the idea of sin. We no longer allow the word in our vocabulary, so we are unconsciously buried by it. We feel guilty for staying up too late again last night, for being so dependent on a wife's opinion, for just having overeaten an overpriced meal once more, for not having read a book for ages, and for not being able to break our habit of smoking.

Communists rushing to be the first to denounce each other have nothing on the West. Americans keep busy trying to get guilt off their backs. One man tries to bribe God with extravagant philanthropy in return for an affair he's having on the side. Another husband substitutes mink for the evenings he has robbed from his wife and showers his children with toys as a payoff for not paying them individual attention. If one splurges today, he will try to make up for it by being Scrooge tomorrow, as the dieter goes without any food the day after a gourmet dinner. Overwork is often an attempted expiation for avoiding time for reflection. Our big hurry is our attempt to hide the utter futility of our life. Often our fanatic involvement in a good cause is fueled by unshriven guilt feelings and not at all by human kindness.

Hindus keep bathing in vain in the Ganges; Pontius Pilate and Lady Macbeth tried washing their hands. Political parties, distinguished nations, and malicious men heave guilt back and forth not getting anywhere—no end in sight. Even dismissing it on the couch as "not guilty" does not discharge it, for we feel guilty with inferiority for having to be psychoanalyzed and for having so little to show for it after all that strain on the budget.

Is this where the altar comes in? Along came a Man who was so different the church has rarely been able to convey that difference even to its own ministers. What Christ did to guilt is still beyond our grasp. This one innocent Man was the very One who graciously took the rap the rest of us are so anxious to evade.

> He took the rap for me, but I don't see what I ever did
> To deserve the rap He says He took for me.
> Or can it be that *that* is the rap pinned on me,
> That I don't see what I ever did to deserve the rap
> He says He took for me?[4]

Moreover, He spent all his days, even His dying moments, forgiving us for this most despicable business of nailing Him. It is hardly enough to call this a watershed in the history of guilt. An atonement remains such a bewildering innovation; but however much our obstinate egotism is repelled by Good Friday, it was God's brilliant move to break the stranglehold of guilt. We waste our time defending ourselves. Christ saved time accepting the consequences on our behalf—His strategy disarms our exhausting rituals of self-justification. "All we like sheep have gone astray; we have turned every one to his own way; and the Lord hath laid on him the iniquity of us all" (Isa. 53:6).

This action brought into being a beautiful alternative to self-defense. This Defense Counsel envelops His listeners in such security they are able to admit to crime; he gives them to understand that they are most acceptable when they fathom how unacceptable they are. The way out of our plight is not in pride and projection; that is the road to hell. Our only hope in handling guilt is to plead guilty and to pray for mercy. Calvary was a revelation of the degraded human heart which beats as much in me as in any man. Any goodness I possess is a gift to be used in shouldering more blame and extending more assistance. Since Christ came, the moot question is no longer "Who is to blame?" but "Take it—it's yours and mine." The question is settled: We were *all* there "when they crucified my Lord." And we'll need more mercy than the next man, for we know too much to get excused by *his* ignorant indifference.

Only the finest spirits have caught this spirit of accepting blame and forgiveness. This is what distinguishes healthy guilt from morbid guilt. Morbid guilt will not accept forgiveness. It was the chief apostle, Paul, who appreciated what an appalling distance lay between him and Jesus Christ when he said that of all sinners he was chief (I Tim. 1:15). It was sincerity and not false modesty that made that shining friar St. Francis say, "Nowhere is there a more miserable sinner than I." The most radiant saints standing nearest to Christ are most sensitive to the shadows on their lives. The man who can't think of anything to apologize for is really sick for lack of this far higher altar.

The night after the battle of Gettysburg, with the remnant

of brave Pickett's charge still moaning on the field, Robert E. Lee was overheard weeping in his tent, "Too bad, too bad." Not until a man is born to such an awareness of his own shortcomings is he in any condition to see any sense in God going to all that expense to send a Saviour. A physician is no use to someone who thinks he is well. Guilt's back is broken only by "a broken and contrite heart" (Ps. 51:17).

Hell is filled with men putting their words into God's mouth: "I'm saved." Humility is superior, although not simple. The insufferable Pharisee thanking God he's "not like other men" (Luke 18:11) is lost, whether he is in church or not. Our own sense of shame will blind us to our neighbor's sins, and bind us to him like a brother. Christ recommended the prayer of a man "who would not even lift up his eyes to heaven" and who cried, "God, be merciful to me a sinner" (Luke 18:13). So Paul Tillich suggests, "The new being is born in us just when we least expect it." Self-satisfied amorality never notices the nobler sense of guilt. "Conscience," as Dr. Carl C. Jung wrote, "and particularly a bad conscience, can be a gift from heaven; a genuine grace, if used as a superior self-criticism."

A man must first die with shame, but not remain indefinitely in self-effacement. He is to confess and come to. Confession is not simply good for the soul, it is indispensable to its survival. It is the only way to remove a deadly poison in time. And while one must not make light of the therapist's capacity to attract these thorns to the surface, the nonreligious counselor is slightly out of character dealing with guilt. Furthermore, the patient may not be able to come to his catharsis without a symbol of authority who forgives in the name of God. The knotty tangle of sin and real guilt may not yield to anything short of the words that exert on that person the strongest sacramental force, at the altar of his fathers, in the temple of his God.

We have erred and strayed from thy ways like lost sheep. We have followed too much the devices and desires of our own hearts. We have offended against thy holy laws. We have left undone those things which we ought to have done; And we have done those things which we ought not to have done; And there is no health in us. But thou, O Lord. . . .[5]

How does this work? A girl of eighteen from a fine old Southern family had a brother twelve years her senior who alternated between bullying her and buying her off with ostentatious presents which he forced her to show off to his guests. He suffered from painful migraines and a succession of other dramatic physical disabilities for which no diagnosis could account. The day came when the brother, desperate for relief from the mounting pressure, found his way to a confessional. In truth, he admitted, he was not this girl's brother, but actually her father. He had regarded that boyhood fornication with rising horror, for he was sure it must be unforgivable. As is so often the case, his whole life had been fabricated from fraud and deceit, with his parents as his accomplices. His social life was blackmail. His whole house was built on lies and frantic additions to stave off the encroaching deterioration. His head was splitting not only from his conscience, but from the inevitability of descending judgment on unworkable behavior.

This does not mean that pathological guilt must not also receive expert psychotherapy. Unhealthy feelings of having committed an unpardonable sin or feelings of strain that do not respond to absolution by the confessor come from the accumulated warp of the years and may require clinical attention. The sick man needs God's forgiveness at the altar as well as the relief which can come on the couch from ventilation of his repression. No man is safe and sound without the experience of grace; and that is never once and for all, but to be continued until that day when God Himself will wipe away the handicap

of temperament from which we shall never till then be completely free.

Nothing but the highest Authority, and the widest offer of
mercy, could have coaxed this hoax from this tormented man.
Nothing short of his hand touching the altar, and another's
hand raised in blessing over his head, could reach the pit of his
despair and spell sufficient hope. Often doctors with a deeper
understanding and a less pretentious faith than self-important
ministers have furnished this superior confessional, but I am
convinced that the guilt and anxiety of such a victim can only
be banished by what to him is the ultimate and the holiest
ground.

I was called to the bedside of a woman who was dying of
cancer. I had known her, slightly, as a sensitive, artistic
person, but she was said to be a little sharp and short with
people. She loved flowers and had often arranged them on
the altar, but she kept her distance from me and never came
to worship services. She was a comparatively young and
attractive woman in her early fifties, but I could see that she
was in misery. Not all her anguish came from physical
causes—her eyes were filled with fear.

One day, after I had made several visits to her, she asked,
"Do you think God can ever forgive me?" Her physical
condition and her tone of voice were enough to melt a heart
of stone. I hastened to assure her of God's unending mercy.
Encouragement was what she needed, what she had been
waiting for. She sat up, grabbed both my hands and choked
out the words, "But I did something horrible!" What came
next was agony for both of us. She was sure that her deed
was so despicable that it would tax my tolerance beyond the
limit, and I could scarcely hear her when she risked that
fateful sentence, "Can I be forgiven?" The answer came,
then and there before my eyes, from the only One who

could give it. He told the dying woman what he told the thief who hung beside Him: "Today shalt thou be with me in paradise."

Her transformation was immediate. Her time on earth was up, but the miracle was that she didn't care. Guilt had pressed her down, and held her there for many years, but in the last days of her life she knew what it was to stand. She was fun to be with, and life was fun for her. She took no more drugs than she had taken before, but she never mentioned pain again. I am positive she was not being stoical— she was new, and everyone around her could see it. A woman had confessed her sins in sorrow, and suddenly there was heaven.[6]

What comes after confession? When the Albatross fell from the ancient Mariner's neck, he found he could sleep. The Mariner's punishment, however, was to confess broadside to everyone upon whom he could fix his hoary eye. Apparently Peter preached often upon what he did to make the cock crow, in order to prove his firsthand knowledge of Christ's power to pull him out of it. Paul's bad record was his bid for attention, too, in order to lead men out to their Damascus Road. The "pitch" of an ex-alcoholic is his own sad story with its happy ending of how God bailed him out. Psychologically, telling on oneself is such a vast improvement over telling others off. Accusation arouses self-defense, while confession is contagious and disarming.

Yet our confession is private, sacred—never to be conducted lightly. Making it to the wrong person could be ruinous. Confession amounts to a holy sacrament and is meant in one sense to be once and for all. Jesus prescribed that the man who said his name was Legion because of the many devils in him, and the woman at the well, tell everyone they met what God had done for them. He advised others to keep it to themselves. God knows what you should do, but our only hope in handling guilt is to plead guilty. Only as we practice understanding and forgiveness can we ever expect to find forgiveness at the feet of Christ.

5
LONELY?

LIFE has given some men such a scare they have withdrawn from society completely and cower in dark corners of mental hospitals covering their faces with fingers of chalk. Guilt is partly responsible for loneliness, but it is difficult for forgiveness to be extended to the isolated. No catalyst can reach these psychopathic hermits. They react spastically to electricity and chemicals, then jerk back to the back wall of the cave of consciousness. They were once frantic, but are now numb, and nothing can bring them to the front door of reality. Charity groups invade these institutions every other Wednesday, but both sides are carefully guarded to keep them from getting involved.

Out in society loners lock themselves on the shelf with bottles for company. Others are concealed in a noisy circuit of cocktail parties. The rejected get lost in addiction in Needle Park, down Skid Row, or serving a stretch in prison. It is hard to find a friend in the middle of a population explosion. Suicide is a way of saying, "Who cares?"

The homosexual is down a hopeless well of loneliness. Perhaps his father ignored him and his mother smothered him. If a girl is a Lesbian, she may have tried to be a tomboy to make it up to a disappointed dad. Now these lonely ones are revolted by the other sex, and heterosexuals in turn discriminate against them in horrified revulsion. The homosexual is estranged from half the race, denied wife and children or unhappy with them if he has them. He is still at the mercy of his deserted and dominating mother. What sick satisfaction he pinches from life takes place under the most humiliating washroom conditions. Emotionally blocked and stunted himself, those friendships he foists even on his own kind are short and sour, frequently flaring with hostile jealousies and morbid cunning. Being a pervert perverts everything, particularly friendship. He lives in fear of blackmail. The life of one of these stillborn men is bitterly lonely. He feels no one who has a home wants a "queer" around. If his plight is known the only hospitality he has stems from his fellow sufferers, who are in no position to offer him what he most deeply craves. He has nowhere to go except into sideshows of anguished sublimation all by himself, or to the mockery of the "gay" bar.

Life is lonely too, for the black man. He is still left out in the cold of so many eating places, voting booths, even rest rooms. He cannot walk in just anywhere. Tragically, he is segregated on sight by everybody. Men divide up into sides to discriminate unnaturally for or against him. He is seldom treated as a regular fellow. He bobs in an abyss of irregularity. He must either wait on tables for the Ku Klux Klan or be a trophy on exhibit at the speakers' table for some organization pushing for civil rights. He cannot be himself or be one of us. He is either scorned as Uncle Tom or exploited as Dred Scott—either refused the floor, or forced to discuss brotherhood. The Negro is not permitted to have any relaxed thoughts on trout fishing or any independent affection for the Republican right wing. Paternalists force him to eat watermelon. Civil-righters forbid it. Traditionalists have him neatly in his place singing Negro spirituals and being waterboy. Liberals promptly amputate him from his rich background. So the Negro is isolated by friend and foe.

So-called friends have made a spectacle of him. They use him as the source of American embarrassment. They direct the new minstrel show, dancing him inexorably as the victim of prejudice. Fighting over the Negro, as we've been doing ever since before Gettysburg, interferes with our fellowship with him. His foes want to condescend to him—to be his big brother. Or a white woman may force the Negro into a more tragic loneliness by marrying him, not for himself, but because she feels compelled to demonstrate how liberal she is. Both rigid traditionalists and dogmatic integrationists are blinded by race; so busy carrying on conflicting campaigns they forget to appreciate each person as something special. A Negro humorist said: "The South doesn't care how close the Negro gets so long as he doesn't get too high. The North doesn't care how high the Negro gets so long as he doesn't get too close." So he is tossed like a football between two opposing forces; any precious black man in *particular* has been scrambled in the feud. We still seek to *own* him. It is lonely for a man who is always given preferment or deferment, for he is never accepted as an equal, but always isolated into a special case, loved or despised because of his racial plight, not for himself.

It is lonely for a child. How many wee ones weep themselves to sleep at night from sheer loneliness. Two hundred thousand abandoned waifs wander homeless on the streets of Caracas, but I wonder if the overprivileged child is not more isolated. The child with everything has nothing without the friendship of his parents. He is kidnaped by a gang of advantages. Intimacy is suffocated under an avalanche of activities.

Think of the terrors of the middle child who is exiled to second place, frightfully lonely because she is always the last one guests notice in the line-up. A beautiful child in the family makes life rough for the others ostracized to the shade. It is terribly lonely to be left out of the compliments. Time after time one girl basks in generous praise: "Say, where'd you get those eyes?" That is a familiar story to the sad little face standing by unnoticed; time after time she goes through this ordeal; always losing out in the battle for attention. We wonder why she's so negative, or difficult—she has much more reason to wonder why she had the raw deal of always being an afterthought.

Parents can slice each child exactly the same sized piece of cake—distribute precisely the same gifts at Christmas—yet despite all the appearance of fair play not be fair at all. For beneath the pretense of equality, the favored boy feels favored —the effect is like silent sunlight. His brother knows with crushing certainty that the look in the mother's eye is not quite so warm, nor eager as when she looks at his brother. We must not be too hard on the mother or father, for it is hard for them to be as warm to the one who is already reacting negatively to the cooler reception life is giving him. Parents are human, and very soon it is difficult to be as positive toward number two even though he needs it more. He rebels all the time, for he senses this difficulty his mother or father has in relating—in identifying with him. The fact that the affection toward him is not as spontaneous is what kills him.

It is also lonely for the child if the mother or father is always putting thoughts in his head—never letting any come out. How remote Junior feels if his private life is never coaxed into the open, for he must always be handing back their image of him. He cannot unload or confide. He must hide everything except the prescribed answers they want to hear.

Sometimes it is lonely because a child is—or isn't—punished. Parents may take pity on the adopted son by not punishing him. He feels discriminated against. The cripple in *Room For One More* was so proud of his first spanking in his new home. "It sure makes a fellow feel regular." The parent cared enough about him to treat him like the rest. Sometimes softness is harsh, as though the child were too hopeless for anyone to go to the trouble of remedial action. Often punishment comes and a child is cut off from the blessed feeling of restoration, or the blows descend without anyone hearing his side or giving his pent-up feelings release. A child suffers in solitary confinement if he is kept in the dark by such inconsistent punishment that he never knows whether it will be skipped or excessive.

The family disapproval must not last long; soon after discipline is administered, precious communion must be restored. More than anyone else in the world the child needs someone who will kiss away the distance he's run away before the sun sets and night falls with him walled off from the world. Jim Backus' heartbreaking solo imagines the lonely boyhood back of Ebeneezer Scrooge's tight fists. In "Mr. McGoo's Christmas Carol" the small Scrooge croons the rejected child's lament.

> You don't know how it feels when you talk,
> And nobody's voice talks back.
>
> A hand for each hand was planned for the world;
> Why don't my fingers reach?
>
> Millions of grains of sand in the world;
> Why such a lonely beach?
>
> Where is a voice to answer mine back,
> Where are two shoes to click to my clack?
> I'm all alone in the world.[1]

It's a lonely life for all of us. The killing pace of the times means more and more that we must remain anonymous. We are seldom among friends, usually lost in

> The sudden solitude in a crowded desert
> In a thick smoke, many creatures moving
>   Without direction.[2]

There are too many cars going too fast for us to wave, even if we could identify one of those flying objects. The junior executive is not welcome at the union meeting, and labor feels out of place dining with management. Everywhere we hear: "I am only a number in a computer to my treasurer. My boss doesn't know I exist—does my minister? I feel exiled if colleges come up in the conversation since I didn't get to go to college. The alumni circle is always cutting me out. My church is streamlining religion into a foreign jargon which bars me from the discussion. I typically feel a frozen asset in others' company. I can't break out of introversion. I am tongue-tied and stranded by these glib 'dialogues.' I drive to work with three other men, silenced by their war stories, since I was 4-F. The family man trots out snaps of his children, but I'm divorced, (or a bachelor). My colleague's youthful appearance makes me feel decrepit. I feel so left out when our neighborhood of big-game hunters get together. Golf separates me into sand traps the size of Siberia. Arthritis has placed me on the shelf."

Others: "Now that I'm successful my old gang won't speak to me any more the same way. They're either jealous or insecure. I can't go back and be accepted as before. They freeze into formality when I come near." Dropouts don't know what to do with a valedictorian. One's big promotion becomes a wedge. "Now they ignore me or apple-polish—they won't just accept me. They either put me on a pedestal or resent being outclassed." A success story is a Greek tragedy in ostracism.

Opposition is isolating. The division of the house hurts communion. Competing for victory rather than for friendship's sake is a study in fragmentation. Industry's struggle for supremacy is not an inclusive operation. Counting off in classrooms to spell each other down may not be teaching cooperation. Someone must end up at the foot of the class, and that will be a lonely spot. The grading curve depends on some poor culprit at the bottom. In all our crash programs slower pupils are lost in the dust. One-upmanship has a high mortality rate, just as being rivals for the same girl will mean loneliness for "Dear John."

Loneliness breeds in secrecy. Isolation is a problem in communication. When husbands and wives begin keeping things to themselves, they drift apart. Dr. Tournier suggests we are constantly carrying on two conversations—the audible one and one with our inner self. In the first, we focus on the weather, the news, or the business that brings us together, but simultaneously we are saying to ourselves: "Will I be late for my next appointment? Will my wife be in a better mood when I get home? What would the doctor think of me if he knew what I said to her this morning?" Or again: "Would my client lose confidence in me if I admitted to him that I don't understand his case at all and that his questions embarrass me greatly?"[3]

Concealing this true conversation is as though each one sends a formal emissary out to carry on small talk—while the real self with his immediate interests is out of sight, talking to himself. Such separate islands feel only the distant waves of each other's influence. They are out of touch, holding each other off at arm's length. Each one acts self-confident, gay, well in hand, hiding from the other the anguish eating at him; his Walter Mitty daydreams of glory or nightmares about his trembling marriage don't dare come out.

Psychiatrists and clergymen so often increase men's sense of loneliness by seeming too secure in their success in self-management. An interview is set up as though one man who can't handle life has gone to one of these supermen to be straightened out. And the fact that the professional will help but needs no help, will listen to a confidence but not confide, thrusts the counselee into more desperate loneliness. Everything about the doctor reminds the patient all the more of odious comparisons. Those two people can never come within shouting distance of each other until the professional somehow admits his mortality. His own failures may befriend his patient far more than his seeming superiority. Loneliness came to an end for one thief on Calvary through his Fellow Sufferer.

Dr. Tournier is a treasure because of his humility.

Over ten years ago, when a friend challenged me to put into practice the Christian faith I professed, the first step that came clearly to my mind was to unburden myself completely to my wife of many thoughts, memories, fears, and failures, which I had never mentioned to her. Such a step seemed impossible to me. I felt I would lose her confidence. We had been very close, and loved each other deeply. We used to discuss everything, even religion. I used to develop for her my pet theories, and she would express admiration and approval. But it is one thing to speak on the level of ideas, and it is an altogether different thing to speak of one's soul. When I took this step, my wife answered me, "Then I *can* be of some help to you!" And she opened up to me in return. We had found the meaning of fellowship. She told me, "Up till now you've been my doctor, my psychologist, my chaplain, more than my husband." In my zeal to help her in her life, my professional vocation had come to hide the person of her husband. It humiliated her by making her into a "case" rather than a wife, and it hindered her personality from coming into full bloom.[4]

There are occasions when a minister must restrain a groom from blurting everything out to his bride before the honeymoon is over. To everything its time. Sometimes a premature confession will precipitate misunderstanding for a brittle or brand-new marriage. If the wife is domineering she may hold the confession over the husband's head like a rolling pin. If he is unstable her confession could be a death sentence. At times, for the present, the church alone, or the trusted physician or faithful friend should hear the confidence. Yet every friendship or marriage of mature minds yearns for the rapport to break the superficial ice and make the escape from loneliness into the blessing of mutual understanding.

How often the minister sees the loss of faith as symptom of secrecy. A wife of five years confessed she didn't believe in God any more and felt absolutely isolated. "How are things with your husband?" "Terrible." She had locked her bedroom door. They had been keeping things from each other until the distance was so great there was no return without a third person, friend to both. Dr. Paul Popenoe tempers the nondirective counseling techniques. He believes that couples often suffer from lack of information about basic psychology, so he seasons listening with education, feeling many people are in trouble because they don't know any better. If one doesn't know what else to do, Popenoe suggests recommending to the husband that he get a baby sitter, send flowers and take her out to dinner—spend the entire evening appreciating her, taking the blame even for failures he can't remember, and reestablish communication with her.

Sometimes one meets a man who's amenable to suggestion. This graying husband had obviously reached that state. His romance was upside down, and he was just too tired and brainwashed to have any more ideas. I recalled Dr. Popenoe's advice, and that night the husband responded with red roses and a French cuisine. His wife had agreed to build him up with all her power too. They both promised me they would spend the time together accentuating only the positive. Somehow that one evening enabled them to resume constructive negotiations and reminded them why they had married each other in the first place. Since another had confidence in them, both gave

it another try. Hostilities diminished. An exchange of compliments got them back into the habit again. And this attention he
paid to her in the intimacy of one evening turned the key in
her bedroom door and switched back on the light of blessing.
Sometimes we suffer in loneliness for lack of one big evening
totally devoted to disarming.

Ultimately any group picture is a desolate proposition until
God is included in it. Without God in the act Romeo and
Juliet can't last. Without this common tie we get lost from
each other. We are children to the end, and children forget,
get things out of all proportion, get sick of themselves, and get
each other wrong. The businessman away all week excuses
himself from church to be with his family, but he's not very
good company without the fresh air of God's more balanced
perspective blowing in now and then. No man can keep a
woman happy singlehanded. So help him God. Certainly the
secret to the weight Christ carried in the lives of others lay in
the solitary re-creation He enjoyed with the Father.

And this experience, of course, casts an entirely different
light on loneliness. A child can somehow weather rejection
from his playmates if he enjoys the right kind of relationship
with his father. Solitude can be sweet with intercession. This is
the answer to Auden's dismal scene of night life where "the
lights must always be on and the music always play." After all,
we are each assigned loneliness. You and I cannot trade places
nor stand in each other's shoes. We do not catch the same
disease at the same time. We are separated. Life is doing
different things to each, and each sees it differently. Death
divides us up. The knothole we must go through has room for
only one at a time and that single-file experience is cold and
biting without warm-blooded belief. God did not promise ex-
emption from suffering, but that he would be *with* us through
it all—we would *not* be alone—"When you pass through . . .

the rivers, they shall not overwhelm you; when you walk through fire you shall not be burned. . . . Because you are precious in my eyes, and honored, and I love you. . . . Fear not, for I am with you . . ." (Isa. 43:2–5). We can conceivably survive brotherless, like Robinson Crusoe, but we cannot live orphaned from the Breathgiver. A well man has made friends with aloneness.

A man cannot be a good brother without first being a good son of God. Think of a Negro minister's story as the ultimate cure from the panic of lostness. The son of poverty-stricken parents dreamed of becoming a doctor. No chance, though, for he was imprisoned on a cotton plantation. Out of his helplessness he prayed to God so earnestly he finally kneeled down in the orange Georgia clay to vow that if God would see him through medical school, he would never let God down. Doors opened, and he made it, and finally was licensed as a physician. One night after a hard day a call for help came to his home from someone critically ill on the other side of the woods. It was two miles away; night had fallen and snow was falling softly. He was too tired to go. He undressed, went to bed and turned out the light. Lying there in the dark he remembered his childhood vow. He threw off the covers, dressed, and set out through the darkness alone. Halfway through the woods a ruffian jumped out of the thick black and in a rough voice demanded the time. The doctor put down his bag and pulled out his watch. Mysteriously, the man vanished and the physician walked on to the bedside of his patient. On his way home at the same place the fellow interrupted him again, this time requesting a match. The doctor reached into his pocket and gave him a match. Suddenly the man was gone again and the physician returned safely.

The next morning the doctor learned that there had been a murder in the woods that night and that a suspect had been caught. He went down to the jail to see who it was. He asked the man behind bars if he were the one who had stopped him to ask the time of day the night before. "Yes." "Did you also ask me for a match on my way back?" "Yes." "Why didn't you murder me?" "Because, each time I came out there was someone else with you."

Why should that surprise those who have been promised: "I will never leave thee, nor forsake thee" (Heb. 13:5)? Myth or history, that is living. Life is unreal estranged from the Ground of its Being. Making friends with one's Maker is life's big idea. "What is the chief end (purpose) of man?" For generations children educated on the Westminster shorter catechism have replied: "The chief end of man is to glorify God and enjoy Him forever." And how can that be unless we begin now? How can we remain lonely enjoying God's friendship?

Are we to be less privileged than the primitives at the point of death? Even the ancient Greeks were ferried across the River Styx. The time comes when we are beyond the reach of human friends—when man can do nothing more for us—Gethsemane, the final break. Then our only hope is an ultimate Hand. Enoch walked with God, and it is said in the Old Testament that Enoch never died. Two little girls were debating this weighty text. One did not understand. The other said, "I do. Enoch walked with God. Each day they walked a little bit farther. Finally, one day they had walked so far together God turned to Enoch and said 'Enoch, this time you are nearer My home than yours. Come home with Me.'" "Out of the mouths of babes" is born wisdom adequate for our alienation and estrangement.

John Donne wrote, "We practice dying by a little sleep," and our daily "good-bys" force us to our prayers to One who will "never leave us nor forsake us." "Suffer me not to be separated And let my cry come unto Thee."[5] That is man's inevitable prayer, though not admitted. This solitary confinement in which we find ourselves—one person to one body—our eyes only under these lids, is not only definitive, but requires us to relate not only man to man but Father to son. Loneliness makes room finally for loving God, and man's closet is rich with this adventure, as the Psalmist found:

> Lord, Thou hast searched me, and dost know
> Where'er I rest, where'er I go;
> Thou knowest all that I have planned,
> And all my ways are in Thy hand.
>
> My words from Thee I cannot hide;
> I feel Thy power in every side;
> O wondrous knowledge, awful might,
> Unfathomed depth, unmeasured height!
>
> If I the wings of morning take,
> And far away my dwelling make,
> The hand that leadeth me is Thine,
> And my support Thy power divine.
>
> If deepest darkness cover me,
> The darkness hideth not from Thee;
> To Thee both night and day are bright,
> The darkness shineth as the light.[6]

6
WEAK?

LIFE IS A moment of weakness. Weakness spawns anger, then guilt, loneliness, fear. Tom Jones couldn't take temptation. Who can? We hear: "I can lose my temper on my way home from church. My impressive New Year's resolutions melt at the first sign of February thaw. 'The evil I would not, I do, the good I would do, I do not.' Here's one Pilgrim who doesn't seem to be making any progress. I am a repeater. I mean well, but I don't have the means to keep the alcohol from going down the same old way, or to hold my tongue even when I bite my lip, or to pull myself together any better than the last time around. I am about where I was last year at this time. My emotions toss me about as though I were a wind sock. Living for me is as reliable as walking on water."

Dr. Tournier has learned that life likes to divide all mankind into "the strong and the weak," a theme he develops in a book of that title. Life becomes a power structure of personalities at home as well as at the board meeting. Guernseys know their place in the line-up as they enter the barn, and they have nothing on us. Domineering bosses ram their viewpoint down the throat of weaker subjects in the pomp of the House of Bishops, or amid the perfumed decorum of the Women's Guild. The strong man is "autocrat of the breakfast table" and tiger to his secretaries. He or she can be velvet-gloved and satin-voiced, but they will be heard and obeyed.

This emotional war horse makes life hell for his psychic inferiors. "When two people live together," wrote Emile

Coué, "the so-called mutual concessions almost always come from the same person."[1] Teamwork is a rare triumph of grace. Usually beneath the screen of courtesy a pseudo harmony exists with someone having had to knuckle under. While the strong man sprawls in his chair, the weak man perches gingerly on the edge. Milquetoast is bottled up under such pressure that he may break and end at the sanatorium.

Most likely the weak man may have a little more crust than Milquetoast—perhaps he's like Micawber or Hamlet, or most commonly the nagging wife and whimpering child. The faint-hearted put up a feeble fight by being negative.

> These protection-reactions are like the safety curtain which is lowered in the theatre when there is a fire on the stage, or the drawbridge that is raised to defend a fortress from attack. Every weak person looks for a shield. It may be the tone of banter or levity under which he hides his distress, or the continual flood of complaints with which the neurotic seems to be warning those around him that his cup is full and that he cannot stand being crossed any more.[2]

Much behavior is really a weak reaction to an unresolved problem. Juvenile delinquency may be a symptom of the youth having had an intolerant father, just as kleptomania may be a form of complaint against an unloving mother. Adultery may be a weak way out from under the tyranny of one's wife.

Being weak does not mean being unintelligent; being at an emotional disadvantage is often an advantage intellectually. The child who is taken advantage of may be drawn into philosophy as were Marx and Freud. Better yet, he may be driven in his despair to God in prayer.

The weak executive may not be so cocksure of himself or have the brass of the talkative type who has all the answers in either black or white. The weak physician will not jump to diagnoses nor be hasty with advice; he sees several sides and appreciates degrees of interpretation. The weak student may not get as high grades as the more assertive, but have a higher I.Q. He will be obsessed by what he doesn't know in the exam, while his strong classmate will be challenged by the occasion and spurred to mobilize his inferior academic forces to better advantage.

The strong and the weak cannot understand each other, and the weak avoid any further symbol of authority over them. The weak son may not join church for fear of having to surrender further to his heavy-handed father. A husband may avoid religion to prevent the head of the house from having one more handle over him. The weak and the strong aggravate each other's tendencies to their mutual destruction.

> Husband and wife cover up their own failings by lecturing each other on those points on which each feels strongest. Also, each attacks and wounds the other at his or her weakest point . . . even without apparent conflict, this drives married couples to counterbalance each other, to their mutual distress; if the wife shows timidity, the husband affects boldness; and the more the latter hides his own worries, the more fearful his wife becomes. If the husband talks about economy, his wife has a wild desire to be extravagant, and the more she spends the more her husband preaches economy to her. The more talkative the wife, the more silent the husband, and the more silent he is, the more she talks to fill the horrible silence. The more loudly the wife proclaims her religious belief, the more the husband hides his own convictions—and the more he hides them, the keener her desire to convert him. The more eager the wife to help her husband in his work, the more humiliated the husband feels, so that he abdicates his responsibilities, and the wife has to take all the more into her own hands in order to save them from ruin.[3]

What makes some men and women weak? We cannot put all the blame on the parents without putting some upon their parents too, and children are predisposed by temperament to react strongly or weakly to the same environment. But if parents are not supremely to blame, they are carriers of this infectious tendency.

Parents seldom love their children for themselves. If the child disagrees or displays different personal tastes, the parent dislikes it and disciplines the child for it. Such overriding egotism is debilitating to a child. Further, the most permissive parents weaken children with withering academic demands. Youngsters are worn down emotionally by being exploited as props to their parents' egos. The child is maneuvered as a pawn who will appear to best advantage to enhance the family front. He is crushed by this weight of parental expectation. His family's strong feelings about the subjects he should study, and the career they want him to enter, sap his energy instead of encouraging him. At school his paper is marked with red checks, impressing upon him the importance of not making mistakes, rather than rousing him to risk the adventure of creativity. He is choked off rather than attracted into open expression. The Parent-Teacher Association is still as negative as Salem without the one redeeming advantage Puritan youth enjoyed—the offer and assistance of a Saviour.

Mothers' and fathers' orders today are not backed up by their belief in the will of God; and such relative "sand" does not seem as sound nor to make as much sense to the children as Plymouth "Rock." The spiritual recession of our time is whittling away at the backbone and the sense of security of our young.

Jaundiced adults have always taken warped pleasure in trampling the native talent for wonder that blooms in childhood. There are angry college professors who love nothing better than to dampen the enthusiasm of bright-eyed classes. Those at a distance from the idealism of youth scorn any sign of hero worship. How many graduates come bristling with criticism out of divinity schools, dedicated to the discrediting of the big names in the Bible or demolishing all institutional churches! This disillusioned clergy cannot wait to inflict their ingenious solutions to the synoptic problem onto congregations who actually may be farther along in the experience of faith. These all-knowing professional smiles do not fortify the next generation. Childhood is an exhausting experience, with nothing *sure* to support one's morals, if the parents' religious moorings are all still at sea on some personal philosophy they compiled at odd moments when they were young. A child is not going to be as strong without a God he can count on and be guided by.

Nothing undermines a child's emotional constitution as much as chronic dissension between his mother and father. It doesn't matter whether there are violent scenes or simply a savage undercurrent of conflict, he senses the situation only too well. The division of the house cannot be hidden from him and he suffers from the split. He is integrated or disintegrated by how well his parents achieve a more perfect union. From birth the child's integration is at the mercy of this marriage. To the extent their union is not truly formed, he will be deformed.

A national assembly of youth was asked to write down anonymously the two questions that meant most to them. The huge majority of both questions was addressed to parents. Their first question was: "Do you love me?" The second question of greatest interest was: "Mother, Father, do you love each other?" A husband asked Dear Abby, "What is the best thing I can do for my children?" She answered correctly: "Love their mother." Nothing can strengthen a child as much as a strong tie between his parents. Nothing weakens him like a weak one. Splitting a home splits the personalities it was in the process of producing. Many of us still cannot make up our minds on the subject on which our parents could never reach an agreement. Their unresolved debate battles on inside the breast of the offspring.

> Dissension between parents leads to a situation which I find repeated in the antecedents of so many of these people crushed by their experience of life that I might call it the classic pattern: Moral abdication on the part of the father, and emotional domination by the mother. In practice the mother suffers more than her husband does on account of the conflict. She has neither the office nor the public house in which to take refuge; so she seeks to fill her emotional void by means of possessive love towards her child. The father holds aloof from the child, taking no further interest in him because he has become the private property of the mother. He leaves him defenseless in the face of what amounts to emotional blackmail by the mother, who dominates the child with her arbitrary demands and her tears . . . the mother makes the child feel that he is hurting her when he does not share all her feelings; she abuses his affection in order to savor his attachment to her, as a balm for her conjugal unhappiness.[4]

This is the unwitting way mothers make their sons homosexual, which is a weakness as well as a loneliness. As the marriage means less the son means more, until her apron strings strangle sex and smother independence. The lad is arrested emotionally short of adolescence—equipped with wings of manhood which will not work.

As much as men may admire the so-called strong, "Strong reactions and weak reactions are both psychosomatic."[5] Tournier's classic illustration tells both sides of the story—a headstrong mother lays down the law in every detail to her two daughters, snuggling them under a blanket of her stifling love well into their teens. One is emotionally smothered in weak reactions and never escapes. She is her mother's pawn, her mother's shadow, a "yes man" in all things. She drives her mother everywhere and never gets married. All differences of opinion or impulses of defiance, any ideas of her own, are repressed. She seems a sweet little satellite, but soon her subconscious mind seethes with smoldering resentment for the independence stolen from her. She escapes into a dream world, suffers from shame at dreams so contrary to her straight-laced life, and outdoes herself trying to compensate for it.

The younger daughter does the opposite, defying her mother on all fronts every inch of the way, flaunting one affair after another, recklessly breaking every moral standard her mother has set—in short, she turns into the kind of person her mother was. She probably proceeds to treat her own daughters as domineeringly as she had been treated, since the strong have such a strong compulsion to show that they are right.

The weak sister has repressed her aggressiveness. This bold one has repressed her conscience and her femininity. Both girls are trying to prove something. Neither is a natural self; they are acting under compulsion—one is weakly acting on her mother's wishes, the other is overreacting against them.

How do we break the swing of this pendulum from strong to weak reactions, back and forth from generation to generation? Modern Freudian psychology represents a shortcoming in handling this power struggle. Freud accused religion of ruining us with neurosis because it only repressed our aggressiveness. Freudian psychoanalysis sets out to free a "Christian" from this unhealthy restriction of his behavior. Certainly this neurotic elder daughter requires insight on her revengeful dreams against her mother. And it will be healthy for her to face up to this and stand up to her mother. However, Christianity asks us to give in freely, not compulsively. The elder daughter had no doubt been misusing Christianity to justify her weak reactions, which were "sickness" from which she needed relief. But, for her to be able to override her mother is no final resting place: simply a necessary step toward forgiveness and reconciliation. The true Christian will be kind not because he is forced to be so out of weakness. His kindness comes by choice from deeper strength and conviction and may be expressed by a "no" as well as a "yes."

Dr. Tournier prescribes correction of psychoanalysis that Christianity has been waiting for.

> Though psychological salvation consists in crossing over from one camp to another [from reacting weak to reacting strong], religious salvation lies in the rediscovery of the divine purpose in which the instinct of life and the moral conscience each have the proper function in the person for which they were designed by God. No doubt that purpose is never fully realized in this world, but case after case has shown that the road to health both for the person and for society lies in a genuine experience of the Grace of God. Such an experience delivers the weak from the toils of their reactions, and the strong from the vicious circle of their strong reactions. It restores the courage of the weak and breaks the pride of the strong. The weak man is reconciled with life, with himself, with his sexuality, with his instincts; the strong men hears the voice of his conscience, and is given a new and different strength, the strength that comes of the recognition of the secret weakness he has been concealing under his appearance of strength. It helps the weak to discern the cowardice in what they thought to be generosity, and the strong to recognize the injustice in what they claimed to be their rights.[6]

We must not confuse Christianity with weak reactions. Just because the weak man is saved by inhibition from the sin of the strong does not make him a saint. Nature and environment assign the stations of the lion and the lamb, and the point is how each one handles his challenge. Unless he is redeemed from his emotional paralysis, the weak man is no finer for "clenching his fists in his pocket." He is no hero who hides his cowardice under the cloak of pacifism. Vowing to be chaste is not a virtuous act if a man is afraid of sexual inadequacy or has never known temptation.

The Bible is by no means a clear-cut handbook of nonresistance. There is no pattern of behavior recommended. Jesus never apologized for scourging the temple with His whip, nor for scalding Pharisees with strong language. The love of Christ is voluntary steel, not forced spongework. Jesus was not cornered in Gethsemane—He stepped into it. The Cross was not an act of coercion, but an act of courage. Christ *accepted* Good Friday as the will of God.

Paul learned from the life of Christ that "We who are strong ought to bear with the failings of the weak . . ." (Rom. 15:1). Christ was merciless toward the powerful. It would be difficult to compose any stronger language than the words with which He addressed the unbending Pharisees: "Snakes," "Blind, leaders of the blind." He addressed the rich unflinchingly: "It is easier for a camel to go through the eye of a needle than for a rich man to enter the kingdom of heaven" (Mark 10:25). He did not say these things to damn the strong irreconcilably to hell, but to crack their arrogance and pull them off the breaking back of the weak, their psychic inferiors.

But to the sick who cried for help and the ashamed who requested forgiveness, Christ was unfailingly full of tenderness and mercy. Never once did He accuse anyone except the proud and unrepentant. To the hurt, the frightened, and the downtrodden—the weak—He was love.

The chastened strong and strengthened weak will discern that each man must find the unique path that leads to God from the place where he alone is standing. Only God knows where that man is, and no Christian may cramp another Christian into his own position. We do not inflict upon another the prescription we received. God will speak to each one directly, not secondhand through us. We are not to oppress a prospective Christian with our spiritual successes, but to love him in such a way as to let him be himself, unfettered before God. He may profit from hearing about some of our problems as he will be nourished by our forgiveness, but he doesn't need us to play God. The humble brother will help most when he permits the man whose time has come to talk. How can love become dominating at the altar if it is uncalled for on the couch? Love is freeing, freeing a man to subject himself voluntarily to God. If the Son shall make you free, you shall be free indeed. When this transformation occurs a man may pose his very personal discovery in Paul's words: "My strength is made perfect in weakness" (II Cor. 12:9).

7
AFRAID?

FEAR IS A friend to rabbit, reindeer, and man in our common struggle for survival, forcing us to be careful crossing the street and reinforcing our defenses with adrenalin. Dr. Harry Emerson Fosdick felt that

> Peril is one of the major stimulants in human history. Scientific medicine has been born of fear. From pneumonia to leukemia and back again, we face dangerous enemies that we are rightly fearful of, and that fact has proved to be one of the strongest stimulants that has ever moved the human mind to great achievement. If someone says that if he had created the cosmos, he would not have made a world where it takes fearful dangers to wake men up, arouse their powers, and marshal their devotions, one can only say that whoever did make the cosmos obviously thought otherwise. For here we are in a world where . . . man has been surrounded by gigantic perils and where the hope . . . of the race depended on those who have won the war of nerves, and in danger have found not paralysis and panic but positive stimulus and incentive.[1]

Fear is not funny when we cannot talk about it. Someone is scared speechless the bomb is about to drop. Big strong men are afraid of heights, of being found out, of saying anything in public, of failure, of being put on the shelf. We are afraid in the hospital, afraid of cancer, of a telegram, of a siren. A child becomes hysterical when the night light is turned off. I have seen that all it takes to reduce a housewife to lip-quivering mute is one anonymous phone call hissing, "Your husband will be killed as he comes home from work tonight." Life and death are enough to make the strongest men cower before they are over. The worst fear is what we don't know and what we can't define, and the fear that singles each out for solitary torture. We wage a war of nerves against our own ghosts of unidentified premonitions. Milton's Satan shuddered:

> And, in the lowest deep a lower deep
> Still threatening to devour me opens wide,
> To which the Hell I suffer seems a Heaven.

A young woman of sensitive face and intelligent mind came tongue-tied to her confessional. She was absolutely unable to recite in class, and it was only with the gravest difficulty that she could make a one-word reply to women teachers. She was able to face this interview only because she was accompanied by the first friend ever to establish contact with her. From the first to the third grades she had been completely mute. Talking had remained a tough assignment. Her conversation with me gradually gravitated back to the day in the first grade where a disturbed teacher was accustomed to terrifying the class to tears. This one girl refused to cry. One day the teacher hysterically waved two train tickets in the air, threatening to take off a member of the class and not return. Again this girl remained the only one who refused to be reduced to tears. The teacher singled her out for this fatal favor. There was a struggle and the teacher struck her repeatedly across the mouth that could not speak after that for three more years.

Resentment, of course, complicated the fear. For years in grade after grade for that girl, the teacher behind the desk would suddenly turn into this other raving maniac, and she would feel rising in her the delayed reaction of wrath against that unfair advantage taken. But it was hostility in retaliation against the pain of terror. Panic had caused the paralysis and occasioned the resentment. She had been frightened out of her anger and her speech.

This fear out of control is a treacherous foe. It can keep a man on the edge of his seat or awake in bed, worry him into neurosis, speed his pulse, wreck his health, wear him down to an early death. Anxiety imagines the worst and magnifies the imperfections of childhood stains upon our lens into monstrous aberrations. Dr. Walter C. Alvarez of the Mayo Clinic in his book *The Neuroses* calls hysteria the ingenious mimic of disease. "The hysterical person is gifted with a great ability to fool himself into illness. He may lose confidence in his ability to move his limbs. The anesthesias are evidently referred out from the brain."[2] Hysteria can be a last-ditch attempt to keep from going into a battle or a marriage. Perhaps the hysteria is a monument to yesterday's failure in this attempt. A man may suffer in such a lack of self-confidence that he develops a psychosomatic symptom such as an ulcer. When fear ruins relaxation, it creates an emotional disturbance.

Fear, like guilt, makes people do dreadful things. Ignorance feeds fear. It fed the fires of the Inquisition and turned the torture rack. Fear of what they didn't know, actually a severe shortage of faith, forced the church to burn John Huss. Fear of free speech and fear of innovation burned William Tyndale, the father of the English Bible, at the fiery stake. Guilt and fear worked together for the Nazis to herd the Jews into the gas chambers. The Civil War was the child of fear. Southerners were afraid of what would happen to their way of life. Both sides lost faith, became afraid of each other, and fought to the death.

Both discrimination and dogmatic demonstration stem from panic. Today in the South the white supremacist piles up into one ugly mass for fear the Negro will take over, and the rioters consume the ghettos of the North. The fear behind the Civil War stalks down the streets of Harlem and Selma breeding crimes of violence in broad daylight. The civil rights situation is explosive with fear, for men huddle into sides, taunt each other with accusations, too insecure to keep off the defensive. Not since a century ago have so many people been unable to speak without raising their voices. Extremists wave frantic flags, so sick from interior fear they are unable to sit still any longer, projecting all the fault on those who refuse to join their effort. So many pitiful people on the militant right and left are unconsciously praying for a rupture rather than the peace of reconciliation. An inner terror has forced them to fix their attention on a foe outside. Their motive is not out of love for their fellow men; they are victims of repressed anxiety seeking distraction in the social tension.

"Perfect love casteth out fear" (I John 4:18). Certainly it greatly helps for the doctor to keep one company during the recollection of the events of wretchedness. Delivery from fear begins with one's escape from isolation. Yet I think this cannot be described exclusively as a technical feat. Coaxing one from his lonely shadows into the sunlight of sharing his existence is an art ultimately known only to love. Security is not simply a science to be learned; it is a maturity that must be gathered from the pooled strength of friends. Only love can pull from the wounded the horror he feels in such a way as to vanquish it forever as a threat.

Such a love is not something the therapist whips up with mortar and pestle; the man who possesses it is *gifted*. It is not something he acquired as a matter of course in clinical training, helpful though that may be; it is granted as a talent. Love has no life apart from the God of love. What we so often call love is nothing but an idle whim of the ego. Unless it is servant of God, it will be sick and selfish.

Fear flourishes deep in the heart of the man to whom life is like living in a rapids approaching the obliterating falls. He is ravaged by a fear that nothing can lay to rest short of religious faith. Dr. Viktor Frankl, the distinguished Austrian psychoanalyst, himself a victim of the German concentration camps, explains how Hitler's hell happened. "I am absolutely convinced that the gas chambers of Auschwitz, Treblinka, and Maidanek, were ultimately prepared not in some ministry or other in Berlin, but rather at the desks and lecture halls of nihilistic scientists and philosophers." When God died, love left, and fear took over.

So much of what religionists have committed in the name of Christianity has been shameful; so often we have declared that "the Lord hath spoken" when actually the Lord hath not spoken. But that past deceit does not permit our partaking in the contemporary blunder of any psychiatry that does not take God seriously and reverently. While it is no secret that there have been charlatans at the confessional, tragedies have also resulted from the reckless counsel of the secular analyst.

The man of God cannot commend the so-called psychotherapy of physicians who dignify an arrogant atheism, such as that illustrated in the incident Bishop James Pike supplies. Such a result has occurred ad nauseum in the name of accredited science when it is really practiced in the name of evangelical nonreligion.

> Several years ago in a large Eastern city, a successful businessman in midlife began to show serious signs of anxiety, with a consequent effect on his health. His physician referred him to a psychoanalyst who readily sensed that a great deal of the man's difficulty came from the fact that over the years he had focused his attention almost entirely on his business, leaving little or no time for other aspects of life, and particularly for recreation. (This is an illustration of how an idol does not cover the whole of life.) The

analyst suggested that he needed a mistress. "But," the patient explained, "I love my wife and have always been faithful to her." The analyst insisted that he needed a "new start" in his emotional life in order successfully to shift his interest from what had been one focus. At length the businessman agreed and a convenient arrangement was worked out.

For a stretch he did feel a good deal better. He found that he could really enjoy life. But he began to be filled with regret that he had not enjoyed life in the years that had gone by. His regret began to take the form of the recognition that his wife, who had been the companion of his youthful labors and who had suffered through the days of privation (he was a "self-made man"), had never had the opportunity to "enjoy life" as he was now enjoying it. As a result of this growing sense of guilt, he began to "take her out" and shower affection on her. The attention to the two women was beginning to take a good deal of time from his business and this was especially serious since over the years he had developed his organization as a kind of "one-man show," never letting go of the reins enough to develop responsible leadership in others in the firm. But his concern for (though not his zest for) his business ever increased now that he was "enjoying life" with two companions. Meanwhile he had developed a real affection for the young lady, and this was now reflecting his interest in a greater attractiveness. He had moved from a simple idolatry (which is called monolatry) to polytheism. Because one god . . . did not "fill the bill," he now had three gods, with no higher deity resolving the conflict among them. He did the only thing he knew to do—and this is a true story—he shot himself. Polytheism in worship leads to schizophrenia (split-personality) in life.[3]

Fear, fundamentally, is felt by those subject to the tyranny of this committee of gods—polytheism. Today's valley of gods may be pills, success, power, wealth, or family, but these dolls are still our gods. One cannot be safely integrated except about the one true God.

So long as our future seems definitely to spell extinction, and a healthier alternative does not remain in question, fear reigns. And to the extent we cannot acknowledge that we suffer from the fear of death, that fear is sick. No patient will be secure if his physician is an opportunist, his wife disloyal, and the policeman on his corner is in the pay of hoodlums. So, if he questions the integrity and dependability of the Source of the universe, he will be as fearful, really, as that poor child who suspects the breakup of his home is imminent, or that pilot who flies a plane serviced and checked out by a notoriously careless mechanic.

Dr. Carl G. Jung explained:

> When I live in a house which I know will fall about my head in the next two weeks, all my vital functions will be impaired by this thought; but if on the contrary I feel myself to be safe, I can dwell there in a normal and comfortable way.[4]

If one is not assured that his life is soundly established against the worst the mortal storm can do, he suffers—and no stoicism nor busy success will be capable of distracting him from this anxiety.

Are not the words of Christ a negotiable option any longer? Has some superior ground been obtained? Then until we have something better to do, why not build here—upon this Rock?

> Whosoever cometh to me, and heareth my sayings, and doeth them, I will shew you to whom he is like: He is like a man which built an house, and digged deep, and laid the foundation on a rock: and when the flood arose, the stream beat vehemently upon that house, and could not shake it: for it was founded upon a rock. But he that heareth, and

doeth not, is like a man that without a foundation built an house upon the earth; against which the stream did beat vehemently, and immediately it fell; and the ruin of that house was great [Luke 6:47–49].

Perhaps the abnormal fear men have of each other has developed because the fear of God has diminished in our lives. The Pilgrim, preoccupied with his divine obligation, was not oppressed by the weight of being alone and helpless against the world. It is terribly depressing to be cornered by fate. Fear obsesses the motionless victim who is not guided by God. The armchair philosopher is a candidate for fright. Panic descends upon those lives trying to sit tight.

Fear is afraid of action. Death and paralysis gradually pick off the men who do nothing about life. The folded fingers in the lap begin to drum, finally to clutch. The secret is to unsheathe our sword and to seek out the enemy, fear. To stand still is to perish in alarm. Life will not allow us to remain philosophers. We are soldiers, and our courage can only handle fear as we advance directly onto the field of battle to engage the enemy. "Let not your heart be troubled: ye believe in God . . ." (John 14:1). That is no idle statement, but a serenity that comes through an *act* of discipline.

Christianity works this way—requiring enough faith for trial. We cannot justify our indecision by waiting until all the facts are in. They are never all in. We must gamble on the best intelligence we have—now. Christ never required more belief from a man than he could honestly offer. He asked of His disciples a fair chance—not for premature pronouncements. That monumental day He walked up the beach by lovely Galilee to call His first four disciples, He did not involve them in theological discussion, He simply said: "Follow me." That fair trial is all faith asks for in the beginning. The day will come when He will ask, "Who do you think I am?" In the meantime, we have our hands full living up to what we already know. We keep our minds off morbid fears by following the best Man we know. "I will trust and not be afraid."

Christ enlists each man. Albert Schweitzer concluded that landmark of his, *The Quest of the Historical Jesus*, with words that have won many men to their assignment:

> As one unknown and nameless He comes to us, just as on the shore of the lake He approached those men who knew not who He was. His words are the same: 'Follow thou Me!' and He puts us to the tasks which He has to carry out in our age. He commands. And to those who obey, be they wise or simple, He will reveal Himself through all that they are privileged to experience in His fellowship of peace and activity, of struggle and suffering, till they come to know, as an inexpressible secret, Who He is. . . .[5]

Psychic health means doing our best, step by step, but includes finally the great admission that so much is up to God. "Having done all," one still stands or falls in his hour of need on the mercy and the grace. The power and the glory sufficient to put away fear are not at man's disposal, but in the hands of prayer. Mendelssohn's *Elijah*, in what I think must be as powerful as music becomes, rests its hope ultimately not in deeds. All that fearful man can do is stand helplessly naked in reverence before God. We do not work our way through a manual. We, too, must wait for "the still small voice" that says: "Be not afraid, thy help is near."

8
YES

THE time comes when you may say "yes" to your life. This means that this embarrassing curiosity of flesh and spirit that wears your name will now enjoy your warm consent. These question marks punctuating our chapter headings have been protecting us from birth. Am I ready now to take that humiliating walk down to the general deposit of mortal disaster and pick out the resentful, guilty, lonely, weak and fearful fool that is I and make the birth-cry, "I'll take *me*"? Life is more than putting up with the situation. Tolerating myself is too halfhearted. *Acceptance* of self means extending a warm *welcome* to whoever I am, whatever comes—wearing my scarlet letter and dunce's cap with just the right pitch of shame and glee—hugging despair close with hope. Paul Tillich's ringing affirmation takes a courage that can come through the marriage of couch and altar: "To accept oneself as accepted in spite of being unacceptable."[1]

Of course, it is common and easier to say "no." So many victims reject themselves and run off with someone else they would rather be. They are afraid creation cheated them, so they try to improve upon the facts by putting on a mask. They do not dare to examine who they are. They will pretend to be whom they please, burying their (resentful, guilty, lonely, weak and fearful) life in a crash program of wishful thinking, at the high price of depression and anxiety. This frantic "no" is a living death. The churches and the night clubs, the suburban "lives of quiet desperation" and the violence erupting in the

slums are choked with those trying to make their get-away
from being themselves.

As Smoke says in "A Cabin in the Clearing,"

> If the day ever comes when they know who They are,
> they may know better where they are. But who they are is
> too much to believe. . . .[2]

Epictetus wrote:

> Remember that you are an actor in a play and the great
> playwright chooses the manner of it. If he wants you to act
> a poor man, act the part with all your powers; and so if your
> part be a cripple or a magistrate or a plain man. For your
> business is to act the character given you and act it well.
> The choice of the cast is another's.

Yes, but—we can't, we won't, always remember this. We
notice what a difference there was between the way Lord
Byron and Sir Walter Scott dragged their club feet behind
them. Byron's burden brewed acid, and Scott wore his infir-
mity with an air of distinction. That there have been so many
men up to Scott makes us say that life is not at the mercy of
circumstances beyond our control, but in the versatility of
man's responses.

True, but we must be aware of how difficult it is for the
very healthiest man among us to accept his life. Do we not
remember what a hard decision it was that night there in
Gethsemane—before Good Friday? I suspect that the temptation at that sore point may have been to "curse God and die."
Our running the risk of being identified will not lead to a soft
life. In some superior way, acceptance is costlier. It is not as
hard to die incognito as on a cross.

Buddhism has a most beautiful way of saying "no" to life.
Nirvana, in the Sanskrit, means extinguished, and the saffron-

robed monk serenely seeks that negative state as the noblest solution to an existence where pleasure plays tricks and pain is predominant. Buddha, after carefully looking life in the face, decided that every desire was damned, so he declined the offer of life in favor of an eightfold path to philosophic suicide. Such a stately refusal should surely chasten any cheap acceptance.

Life must be embraced with the understanding that we do not understand most of it. And there will be occasions when Buddha's policy will appear superior to the most enthusiastic positive. For accepting oneself involves more than confessing fury, pleading guilty, and refusing to repress our fears any more. Christianity's sweeping "yes" takes into account the ambiguity and irrationability of the entire shock of our suffering. Absolutely nothing must interfere with our intention to go this "second mile" that Christ initiated. Life is larger than any life view and will stretch each man before it is through with him.

Honesty is a stiff assignment, yet the secret to this is to start from scratch. Our life is our response to a given situation. Everything depends on how we make out when all our material props and emotional supports are whipped out from under us. Life at its deepest level must learn how to cash in on its disadvantages. We are not simply to weather the forces of destruction, but recruit them for our use. We can, of course, die in a state of arrested development, begrudging our lack of good looks or low I.Q. Or we can have a tantrum during our time on earth, snarling viciously at every turn of the screw along with Clarence Darrow: "Life is an unpleasant interruption of nothingness." But we want to make clear that if we decide in favor of faith, there is no such thing as an easy way out. If we are fully awake when we say "yes" it will make our lip quiver, and before it is over we will lose our faith in order to find it many times. Our highest mountains have their contrasting valleys, as brightest days do nights. The bravest knight must take the hardest position on the field of battle, believing still when all belief has fled, patient and forgiving still after all is lost and God seems dead. And when one's voice is gone, one must still whisper "yes" as did Robert Louis Stevenson, "I believe and though I woke in Hell, would still believe."

The time comes when we no longer know where we are, whether we have faith or not—we must finally find that humility to leave our lack of faith up to Him who is faithful in our faithlessness. Our belief, our integrity, our hope, cannot save us. We are eventually, when our time comes, completely at Another's mercy. Paul Tillich rested his final words in *The Courage to Be* beyond the reach of effort. "The courage to be is rooted in the God who appears when God has disappeared in the anxiety of doubt."[3]

Tolstoy despaired of ever finding a satisfactory answer in books or among men who felt themselves afflicted with intelligence. He turned to the peasants and their simple childlike faith. This reminds me of my great-aunt Em, who manifested the most distinguished religio-psychiatric understanding of anyone I know. Another person would have grown bitter over the child labor imposed upon Aunt Em as a little girl. She would not permit the drudgery to be an imposition. She went to meet her challenge with words brightly polished by the time she used them on her dying day, "This will do me a world of good." Her prayers were fervent pleas for mercy on her own "multitudinous sin," and added to her humility she possessed the amazing capacity to adjust flexibly to life's surprises. She was enabled to take whatever befell her as a personal favor from the hand of One in whom she believed "*all* things work together for good."

The book of Job is not one man's biography or play; it is the very same crucible through which we must each go. Life becomes the spectacle of the best man trying to do right against everything turning out wrong. We can admit we are fools, agree to be ourselves, and say our prayers, but life won't take our word for it. At what point will Job break? How about you and me? His funds are taken away first, then his business, his home next, then his children, and finally his health. If life doesn't take these things from you, one by one, death is going to do it all at once. Can we accept these facts of life?

Job was wrecked by these merciless disasters crashing down unaccountably upon him. He raged with the unfairness of it, his brain was crazed with the question, "What did I ever do to deserve all this?" He kicked over every stone in his vain search to find the reason for his "outrageous fortune." Every answer only multiplied more maddening questions. Then one day, in the excavation misery had made, God arrived. Rather than his continuing to bombard God with the tantrum of his invective "Why?" everything was changed, and the questions melted before such "nearness to tremendousness." Something incredibly beautiful happened to a Job transfixed by what he called, "things too wonderful for me. . . ." (Job 42:3). No longer would he treat earth as a curiosity shop to get to the bottom of. He had advanced into a mystery. "I have heard of thee by the hearing of the ear: but now mine eye seeth thee" (Job 42:5). Some scholars delight in pointing out that later editors must have doctored the tragedy of Job into turning out well. But God always enters life unexpectedly just as Job portrays it. For those who believe in a God who comes in time to make man's cup run over, the book of Job rings true as it is. It reminds us of how beautifully things turned out because of the way another Man accepted His Cross. It opened a grave that made room for a resurrection.

Nothing can integrate us satisfactorily short of the experience of God. We are still saying with Augustine, "Our souls are restless, our souls are restless, until they find their rest in Thee." Man may need the rest and relief the couch can offer, but his life cannot be fulfilled until he falls before the altar of God.

Communion with kindred spirits cultivates the self-acceptance leading to God. When can the church recover even as much of its original self as Alcoholics Anonymous? Like Peter and Paul before him, the AA member assigned to give the "pitch" confesses his own defeats. He does not berate or scold, but disarms his hearers with his own helplessness. Here is no dogmatic high-pressure theological salesman giving condescending advice. He invites his colleagues to laugh with him at his folly, and cries his terror out to all their hearts' content. Such a climate is not competitive, but companionable. When will the pulpit recall Peter's self-condemnation for his denials, or Paul's admission of his guilt after Damascus? With the establishment of such rapport, "one beggar is able to tell another where to find bread," without accusing each other.

The church need not be formal to be at its best. "For where two or three are gathered in my name, there am I . . ." (Matt. 18:20). Two are enough to give and take, to discover who you are, and find "Our Father who art in heaven. . ." (Matt. 6:9).

In the spring of 1965, I heard several lectures by Paul Tournier. Gray-haired and bent from age and illness, he held his audience spellbound, although speaking through an interpreter. He concluded his remarks with a personal experience which I offer as an illustration of the operation of grace. He was an orphan boy who had had great difficulty being accepted and accepting himself, and the first significant step in this experience was the interest which his Greek professor took in him. The professor was not a religious man, but invited lonely young Paul into his home and into his intellectual world. "He reinserted me back into humanity." While their intimacy never ranged beyond the exchange of ideas, it represented a great stride for them both. Many years later, long after Dr. Tournier had become a Christian, he cast about in his mind for some friend who might read and offer suggestions on his first manuscript before it went to the printer, and he thought of his old Greek professor, now retired. The professor agreed and asked Dr. Tournier to read the first chapter to him. When the chapter was completed and Dr. Tournier looked up for a critical reaction, the old man said merely, "Paul, continue." He read another chapter. "Paul, continue." He read the third chapter. Then the old teacher said, "Paul, we must pray together." They prayed. Afterward, Dr. Tournier exclaimed, "But I didn't know you were a Christian." "Yes." "When did you become a Christian?" "Just now."

As long as we live we shall be hateful, guilty, lonely, weak, and afraid. This accounts for our continued interest in assistance. That first helping of grace introduces us to a steady diet. Baptism is only a beginning. Christians are forever sinners, but their distinction is in knowing it and knowing where to find the relief and courage to keep reorienting, repenting. Pride poisons the non-Christian unawares. The convert sins in pride too, but he knows it and knows the refreshment of forgiveness over and over again.

The Christian born to this new security can bear to acknowledge his resentment. The man who knows he will be shown mercy can bring himself to recognize and plead more guilt than the frightened man would ever find. The Christian is lonelier, perhaps, but is sustained by this standing offer that redeems unbearable exile by the repeated touch of the Master. Weakness is strength, fear is friend to a pilgrim who is turned by them to God.

Our ultimate health lies not in introspection but in adoration of this One whose life gave a beautiful reception to the ugliest events. He accepted the unmentionable Cross in such a way as to make it indispensible. He regarded other's heartbreaks with moving compassion, He bore His own torture, mockery, and murder so modestly. He assumed death was life, and felt the end of the world would be an improvement, and the beginning of a better one. The grave, from His point of view, was the perfect place to hold the Resurrection.

At the feet of this strange Figure, so distant, yet nearer than we are to ourselves, the couch and the altar are one.

9
WHAT WILL BECOME OF ME?

WHILE ANALYSIS or confession is necessary, either can also pervert the past out of all proportion, fossilizing the patient back there. "Analysis helps the patient to avoid the neurotic identifications and projections which he has carried over from the past, but it may hinder his responding to the unique and unexpected in the real present. Analysis may turn the patient backward upon himself."[1]

The counselor is not only to be the ghost of Christmas past, but a colleague, sharing, connecting, creating a *now* to prepare the best way for Christmas yet to come. "In my end is my beginning," said Mr. Eliot later on in "East Coker." "Therefore if any man be in Christ he is a new creature: old things are passed away; behold, all things are become new" (II Cor. 5:17).

Paul Tillich remarked in *The New Being:*

> The counselor and the psychiatrist can *help;* he can liberate us, but can he make us whole? Can he give us salvation? . . . They cannot because they themselves need wholeness and are longing for salvation. Who heals the healer? . . . It is the humanly incredible, ecstatic, often defeated, but never conquered faith of Christianity that this new reality which was always at work in history, has appeared in fullness and power in Jesus, the Christ, the healer and Saviour.[2]

Psychological salvation consists in unburdening oneself of his bottled feelings. As soon as he perceives these causes of his compulsions and inhibitions and brings fresh confidence into play, he is pronounced cured in the clinical sense. The secular doctor is satisfied once the formerly dominated boy talks back to his dad. He emerges from his depression when he rises from his submissive posture as the doormat to stand up for his rights. This is enough for the scientist. His patient successfully returned to the scene of the crime and has now come back armed with insight and strength.

Yet recovering from *sick* guilt does not absolve one of the *real* guilt with which it is inextricably entangled. A man can get rid of unhealthy fear and still be scared to death. It is good for a victim finally to be enabled to get angry at the outrages perpetrated on him before he was big enough to do anything about it; but he is not safe and sound until he is equal to the challenges of "forgiving all that is past" and truly accepting the way things have to be. And until he reaches that sublime maturation point, he is still a sick and haunted man.

There are those who must be taught to lose their temper. How can one control a temper he's afraid to try? But while most psychologists will leave him there at the end of that elemental lesson, that is not the end of it; there remains the larger lesson of its keeping. As soon as one has shed pathological guilt, he is then faced with the vast assignment of accepting a lion's share of blame seen by the light of Someone supremely innocent who assumed a cross.

What is one's ultimate responsibility toward those who have hurt him so terribly? The strict psychologist may not care about his patient's marriage and the other suffering members of his family. The patient must. Surely one's only hope is not in endlessly retaliating with the same aggressiveness they misused on him. He must finally rise above that essential fight for his rights for a higher calling. No one will ever arrive at the happy estate where he enjoys good health until he spontaneously transcends the healthy selfishness to make "the gift outright."

Something we were withholding made us weak
Until we found out that it was ourselves.[3]

Indispensable to each man's triumph over the little man in
him is the assistance of that One the mature can admit is a
Saviour. The world has done Him grave injustice by painting
Him with pointing finger. He greeted no man with reproach
—except the proud. His approach to the hurt is summed up
spaciously in two words: "Judge not." He objected to throw-
ing stones and was never guilty of giving good advice. He even
preached in parables in such a manner as to permit His audi-
ences to decide for themselves with which character to identify. He was a man of mercy; scolding is an alien adjective
projected on Him by the squirmers in the scorner's seat. In His
story, the shepherd rejoiced on the recovery of his lost sheep.
The wayward one was returned to the favored seat "on his
shoulders" with not so much as one "I told you so." His father
ran to sweep the prodigal into his waiting arms while the *son*
was still "a great way off." The father's giant strides ate up all
the distance time and pride had put between. And when the
boy confessed, the father quickly kissed his guilt away, absorbing all that heartbreaking pain in a banquet of gifts, turning
doomsday into the light of homecoming. The Master Psychotherapist railed solely against the proud; for the humbled
He was "so slow to chide, so quick to bless." The mercy of
modern science and the practice of our pews have not yet
come within shouting distance of the quality of mercy of this
Man who wept over Jerusalem and who promised the penitent
harlots they would surely come into His heaven ahead of the
rest. His was a therapeutic spirit.

We have already acknowledged the prerequisite faith of the
client in coming to his counselor. Consider the effect of the
counselor's faith in God. Then the ceiling of the interview is

heightened in readiness for greater expectations than any god-less interview has a right to expect. The client has not simply come—he was sent. This sufferer will not be a similar case, but unlike anyone else who has ever been in that conference room before. The confessor is not in control, nor the patient. What happens is out of their hands, and as Buber has already warned, the procedure, the timing, and the results will be singularly unparalleled. Patience will be stretched to the breaking point, repeatedly. Fear and despair will rear their ugly heads to panic such a confidence. Yet there is an exciting promise to those who will run the risk of waiting—"upon God." And the counselor hangs on through the strain of grinding teeth— "Why did this incorrigible have to come to me?" "How did I ever get into such a thankless business?" "I shall refer this recalcitrant." Then, without warning, the water gushes out of rock and takes our breath away. So often when the relationship seems stagnant and mutually harmful, it reminds the confessor of prayer and suddenly the deadlock is broken and the friend-ship flushes with health. The confessor is aware for "one brief shining moment" that he is not, after all, self-employed.

No one knows the fantastic secret Jesus exercised to inte-grate the pathological brute among the tombs who had so many devils he named himself Legion. The sudden restoration to sanity of someone so sunk in psychosis as that demoniac from the city of Gerasa stuns us with disbelief. Yet, Jesus insisted, ". . . greater works than these shall [ye] do . . ." (John 14:12). I must not imply that I have in any way plumbed these mysteries, but in all honesty I think I know the direction in which his power lay. Art critic A. B. Neumann, one of the great men of modern times, scrawled a penciled note as he lay dying: "What we all want to know about great men we admire is whether they really care for us." And in the shadowboxing conversations, the furtive, fleeting glimpses we get and give of our interiors, this caring is what we are all after.

Each lonely sufferer is seeking piteously of his physician: "Can you really care what happens to me—a little?" Behind the cold face of professionalism or beneath the pretense of banter, we all wear our hearts upon our sleeves—sick with wanting, hiding, baring this search. The analyst may dismiss it, the confessor may put on theological airs, but the action of healing has to do with the *reality* or *unreality* of someone's love. Therapy cannot take place in a sterile field. All is empty prattle on the patient's part unless he has caught the creative note of another person actually affecting him with friendship.

It goes without saying that the Lord "healeth the broken in heart, and bindeth up their wounds" (Ps. 147:3). But that must be administered in the flesh. Elisha could not resuscitate the inert boy by sending his servant. The boy did not come to until Elisha was with him, eye to eye and mouth to mouth. Not until the forlorn victim of gross neglect has made connection through someone's involvement is he brought in out of the cold. I believe a man must suffer from analysis until such re-creating brother's love offers a synthesis.

For caring is the only life, and our patient can only catch it from our caring, as we could only have caught it from another in that golden chain reaction, streaming from the splendor of that anchor Man, "We love, because he first loved us" (I John 4:19).

To go back now and pick up how this applies to who I am—another man about to go under the anaesthetic had the courage to share his cowardice. He admitted he was afraid and needed help. That honesty permitted prayer and made room for another person to share the load of fear. Under the anesthetic the doctor found him calm and peaceful.

C. G. Jung reported that during interviews that man in the

nightmare we introduced in the first chapter gradually dredged up his worries, and as they came to the surface and were ventilated, the pressure below was relieved. Finally, the man's dream improved. It started as the same dream—the monster emerged—but the man escaped, a sign he was no longer in imminent danger of going under, but competent to bear the strain, since the enemy was identified and the burden shared.

When am I going to be myself? Perhaps your fifteen-year-old daughter has been a brooding storm center of quixotic behavior. She has been a walking civil war, impossible to deal with. Suddenly she blooms. Where did this lovely angel come from? You are suspicious—surely it is but the calm before the storm. To your consternation peace continues. The point is, someone has been noticing her at school. You had despaired of an unruly black sheep—perhaps had come even to begrudge her existence. Then along came someone who thinks she's "something." And that one boy's confidence in this wild girl-woman may have accomplished an integration.

"Help somebody be somebody." Merely giving someone something won't do that. Charity can remind a nobody that that is exactly what he is, but paying him attention, appreciating him, showing confidence in him enough to consult *him* matures him. It is appreciation, not persuasion, that puts a man on his feet. How many convicts have gone straight—not out of fear of further punishment—but because as one said, "I just can't let the judge down"? How can a man get hold of himself if someone else won't trust him until he can learn to trust himself?

This was Christ's approach. He never saw a man at his worst, but at his best. Jesus saw troubled Zaccheus as he could be, would be—giving himself to God. Zaccheus had literally been out on a limb, but standing on the rock of Jesus' confidence in him, he was re-created. Zaccheus saw himself for the first time reflected in Christ's eyes. The lid of past limitations was off. Sitting there eating with this Christ he wondered, could Christ really be right? Zaccheus rose to the occasion not simply a new man, but as one who came to himself for the first time. The real Zaccheus stood up, stripped of all the tattered trappings of insecurity and fear. He was becoming the man God had in mind and meant him to be. The secret of our true identity is not in introspection, nor endless analysis, but in the splendid sublimation—Christ's vision of us.

Jesus looked on a handful of ragged fishermen and saw apostles—until finally they did too. Jesus saw more to the woman at the well than just more husbands, and with that rich encouragement she broke loose from a past that was out of character. A thief on a cross looked into the eyes of Someone suffering companionably at his side (not across a frightening expanse of desk) and for the first time realized he was not a worthless thief—the Man hanging in the middle thought enough of him to give His life. When that deed is understood it dissolves the inferiority complex. When one personally learns why Jesus went all the way to Golgotha, power is released and in this Presence he is redeemed and restored to his rightful mind. That perfect love casts out the fear of being, and gives us what Tillich calls *The Courage to Be*.

Christianity does not blot out individuality, but brings it to flower. When Paul became Christ's he became *more* like Paul, not less. "Make me a captive, Lord, and then I shall be free." There is far more variety and refreshing contrast in the disciples after Christ made his impression on them than in the half-hearted manner in which they lived before that reveille. Under the devil's influence we remain in the anonymous woodwork. When we're afraid, we bluff, merging into the crowd. In the insecurity of a world rigged against us we play with poker faces. Communism forces men into masses, dictatorships are too much on the defensive to tolerate distinctions. Only among the children of a God who fondly created each, can one safely show his true colors. But if this is my Father's world, then I . . . could it be that I am to be incredibly distinguished?

Who am I? A number? An animal? An orphan? A conditioned reflex? Who is Jesus? Son? What does that make us? Related not so much to the dirt as to God? Does this make the other fellow my beloved twin? "Behold my children it doth not yet appear what we shall be, but we know that when He appeareth we shall be like Him, for we shall see Him as He is." Someday at the end of the straight path we shall find out who we are. We shall be walking homeward as one boy in a parable you remember, lonely, rejected, traveling incognito, and suddenly a great crowned and shining figure shall step out of the shadows and sweep us into His arms, and He shall say in answer to our quest of the years, kissing away our frantic tears: "My son, my son." "And then we shall know even as we are known."

> And all shall be well and
> All manner of thing shall be well
> When the tongues of flame are in-folded
> Into the crowned knot of fire
> And the fire and the rose are one.[4]

NOTES

Preface

1. "The Origin and Development of Psycho-Analysis," *Great Books* (Chicago, London: Encyclopedia Britannica, Inc., 1952), Vol. 54, p. 1.

2. C. G. Jung, *Modern Man in Search of a Soul* (London: Harcourt, Brace & Company, Inc., 1933), p. 130.

3. Martin Buber, *Between Man and Man* (London: Routledge & Kegan Paul, Ltd., 1947), p. 184.

4. Paul Tournier, *Médecine de la Personne* (Neuchâtel and Paris: Delachaux & Niestle).

Chapter 1

1. Sigmund Freud, *The Basic Writings of Sigmund Freud* (New York: Random House, Inc., 1938), p. 77.

2. *Ibid.*, pp. 75, 76.

3. *Ibid.*, p. 109.

Chapter 2

1. *Ibid.*, p. 7.

2. Søren Kierkegaard, *The Journals of Kierkegaard* (New York: Harper Torchbooks, 1958), p. 136.

3. "Sigmund Freud," *Great Books* (Chicago, London: Encyclopedia Britannica, Inc., 1952), p. 16.

4. *Ibid.*, p. 18.

5. *Ibid.*, p. 19.

6. *Ibid.*, p. 84.

7. Maurice S. Friedman, *Martin Buber; The Life of Dialogue* (New York: Harper and Brothers, 1960), p. 187.

8. Søren Kierkegaard, *op. cit.*

9. "It is the surpassing merit of Jones's study of *The Life and Work of Sigmund Freud*, and especially of the last volume . . . that instead of piling up worshipful epithets, it *shows* us Freud's

courage and humor, his tenacity and tolerance, his attitudes toward his disciples and his own works, his response to suffering, fame and death. We are made to live through his troubled relationships with Otto Rank and Sandor Ferenczi and savor greatness as we read the detailed and wise letters to Ferenczi in which . . . few men were so memorable." *From Shakespeare to Existentialism*, Walter Kaufmann (Garden City, New York: Doubleday & Co., Inc., 1960).

10. Quoted in Friedman, *op. cit.*, p. 187.

11. Martin Buber, "Heilungaus Der Begegnung," *Neue Schweizer Rundschau*, xix, Heft 6, Oct. 6, 1951, pp. 382–386.

12. Paul Engle, *A Woman Unashamed and Other Poems* (New York: Random House, Inc., 1965), p. 39.

13. Friedman, *op. cit.*, p. 182.

14. Quoted in *ibid.*, p. 194.

Chapter 3

1. Ernest Gordon, *Through the Valley of the Kwai* (Philadelphia: Westminster Press, 1961).

Chapter 4

1. Malraux and Baruk quoted in Paul Tournier, *A Whole Person in a Broken World* (New York: Harper & Row, Publishers, Inc., 1964), p. 15.

2. *Ibid.*, p. 133.

3. T. S. Eliot, *The Complete Poems and Plays* (New York: Harcourt, Brace & Company, 1952), p. 361.

4. "For Heaven's Sake!" The North American Ecumenical Youth Assembly, Kromer & Silver, 1961 (recorded by Union Theological Seminary, N. Y.).

5. *The Book of Common Prayer.*

6. D. A. Redding, *Psalms of David* (Westwood, New Jersey: Fleming H. Revell Co., 1963), pp. 54–55.

Chapter 5

1. "Mr. McGoo's Christmas Carol" (N.B.C., 1964).

2. T. S. Eliot, *op. cit., The Family Reunion*, p. 235.

3. Paul Tournier, *Escape From Loneliness* (Philadelphia: Westminster Press, 1948), p. 44.

4. *Ibid.*, p. 46.
5. T. S. Eliot, *op. cit.*, "Ash-Wednesday," p. 67.
6. *The Psalter Hymnal*, United Presbyterian Board of Publications, 1927, p. 275.

Chapter 6

1. Quoted in Paul Tournier, *The Strong and the Weak* (Philadelphia: Westminster Press, 1963), p. 141.
2. *Ibid.*, p. 110.
3. *Ibid.*, p. 159.
4. *Ibid.*, p. 48.
5. *Ibid.*, pp. 27, 28.
6. *Ibid.*, p. 34.

Chapter 7

1. Harry Emerson Fosdick, *Living Under Tension* (New York: Harper and Brothers, 1941), pp. 21, 22.
2. Walter C. Alvarez, *The Neuroses* (London: W. B. Saunders Company, 1951), p. 308.
3. James A. Pike, *Beyond Anxiety* (New York: Charles Scribner's Sons, 1963), pp. 12, 13.
4. C. G. Jung, *op. cit.*, p. 129.
5. Quoted in Albert Schweitzer, *Out of My Life and Thought* (New York: Henry Holt & Co., Inc., 1949), pp. 56, 57.

Chapter 8

1. Paul Tillich, *The Courage to Be* (New Haven, Conn.: Yale University Press, 1952), p. 164.
2. Robert Frost, *In the Clearing* (New York: Holt, Rinehart & Winston, Inc., 1962), p. 17.
3. Paul Tillich, *op. cit.*, p. 190.

Chapter 9

1. Friedman, *op. cit.*, p. 189.
2. Paul Tillich, *The New Being* (New York: Charles Scribner's Sons, 1955), pp. 40, 41.
3. Robert Frost, *op. cit.*, p. 31.
4. T. S. Eliot, *op. cit.*, "Little Gidding," *Four Quartets*, p. 145.